*The Story of a Beloved World Traveler*

# AL BELL
# *Remembered*

*By* Becky Bell-Greenstreet

© **2010 by Becky Bell-Greenstreet**
58837 Old R.R. Grade Rd., Coquille, OR 97423

*All rights reserved.*

No part of this book may be reproduced or utilized in any form or by any means, electronic or mechanical, including copywriting and recording, or by any information storage and retrieval system, without permission in writing from the author.

ISBN: 978-0-9819363-4-5

Printed in the U.S.A. by
Wegferds Printing & Publications - North Bend, OR

# "Huckleberry Pie"
## Written and composed by Al Bell

(REFRAIN)

I like Huckle buckle, B – U – buckle, buckle
I like Huckleberry pie.

H – I – Hickle, dickle, B – I – Pickle dickle
That's the reason why.

No matter what – kind of pie you say has stood the test
There will always be one pie to me that is the very best!

G – O – Goozleberry, R – A – Razzleberry
Pies that make you sigh.
I like Hucklebuckle, B – U – buckle buckle
I like Huckleberry pie.

Now some folks crave a lemon pie
With frosting on the top
And others say that apple pie
Is the pie that hits the spot
But no matter what kind of pie
About which you'd like to boast –
There is only one kind of pie
I like the very most!

I like cherry, derry, I like blackle-berry
I like strawzleberry pie.
I like peachel-deeple,
I like apple-dapple,
Chiffons that reach the sky.
But of all the different kinds of pies
About which you'd like to boast –
There is only one kind of pie
I like the very most!

Oh! I like…(Refrain)

# Introduction & Acknowledgements

This book was written expressly for devoted Al Bell fans. If you are not familiar with my father and his career, you may not appreciate or understand why Al Bell had fans in the first place. Between you and me, when it came to experiencing my dad giving his assembly programs…well… you "kind of had to be there." However, as you read this book, I think you will appreciate the extraordinary personality and accomplishments of the phenomena that was Al Bell.

This book has been in my head and on yellowed tablet paper and assorted scraps, notes, and un-paragraphed pages (done on an old Smith Corona manual typewriter) for too many years. Because of people like Doug Johnson who lit the fire on his "Blue Skunk Blog", Renae Barkema, creator of the Facebook page "I Remember Al Bell", Jim Calkins and nearly 3,000 dear souls who responded to that page, and Mike Kilen who wrote an article for the Des Moines Register that clinched the deal, I picked up a half-finished manuscript, and set out to answer as many of your questions as I could.

First, I addressed questions like "How did he get into this business?" and "What was he like at home?" Some of you were curious as to Al Bell's health issues. Many of you mentioned the animals he brought to your schools. A large section of this book is the transcription of my father's recorded autobiography (his first twenty years). He taped this information while living in Ankeny, Iowa circa 1974 to 1975. Frequently, I would sit nearby with a notebook, prompting him and asking questions. He made those cassette tapes so that I could write this book someday. Sorry it took so long, Daddy!

Many of you have traveled abroad, and a few of you even live abroad. Some of you have said your desire to travel and live in faraway places was inspired by Al Bell, so, I've addressed why I think he made such an impact on so many of you. As far as specific questions regarding my parents' trips abroad, I wasn't there. In some cases, I'm not old enough to have known about some of those adventures. In most cases, I don't and can't remember all of their wonderful stories and anecdotes from around the world. So, I have focused here on my trips with my dad and the many memories I have of him.

If not for Liz Gilman of Gilman Media, Inc., who contacted me regarding a possible "Al Bell Film Festival", I would not have had the opportunity to present this book to a large audience. I can't thank Liz enough for organizing and co-ordinating this event for all of us – especially for me, and for my siblings and their families. Liz has the patience of Job, and she needed it to bring it all together. Thank you, also, to the White Pole Road group who, through Liz's connections, sponsored the event. We appreciate the folks at the Saints Center in Stuart, as well, for providing the perfect location in the heart of our hometown area. For almost twenty years, Al Bell's address was Rural Route, Stuart, Iowa.

Thanks to Andie E. Jensen, friend and local author, who happened to have published his second book on the history of law enforcement in Coos County, Oregon, just as I was searching for a local printer. Andie led me to sparkling Edi (originally from Iowa!) and her creative daughter, Karen, of Wegferds Publishing in North Bend, Oregon.

Thank you to my dear friends who have encouraged me with my writing and specifically, this project: "Curly" (Carole) Schneider, Diane Knight, Wendy MacDonald, and Lynn Danner. And hugs to my very dear friend, Pat Eichhorst, who volunteered her professional copy-editing skills to as many of these pages as possible.

My dear sister, Rhea, who holds more stories about our dad in her head than anyone, has supported me faithfully in this challenging endeavor. My brothers, Allen and Doug, threw the baton to me willingly and in good faith. I have represented our parents and family as accurately as I could. I'm sure there are a few discrepancies regarding dates and details. Thanks for trusting me with these memories made public.

I thank God for my very best friend and supporter, my husband, Daryl. My mother used to refer to herself as Daddy's "sounding board." Daryl let me talk about this project for years until I was ready to tackle it. A writer himself, Daryl gave me just enough input and plenty of encouragement for me to follow through this time.

Most of all, I wish I could thank my father and mother for giving me such a unique life. In spite of the many times during my growing up years when I wished my parents were normal, I've always been proud of what they did for Iowa's school children. I wish they could read all the testimonials and thank you's on Facebook. And though I've sometimes wished that I could be normal, I have since thanked God for being, I hope, "a chip off the old blocks." My parents gave me such a hands-on liberal arts upbringing, that I could never decide what I wanted to be: singer, actor, musician, writer…How wonderful to have such options! The Lord has given me awesome blessings. Thank you for picking up this book.

Al Bell on the job with a tour guide on the Nile River.

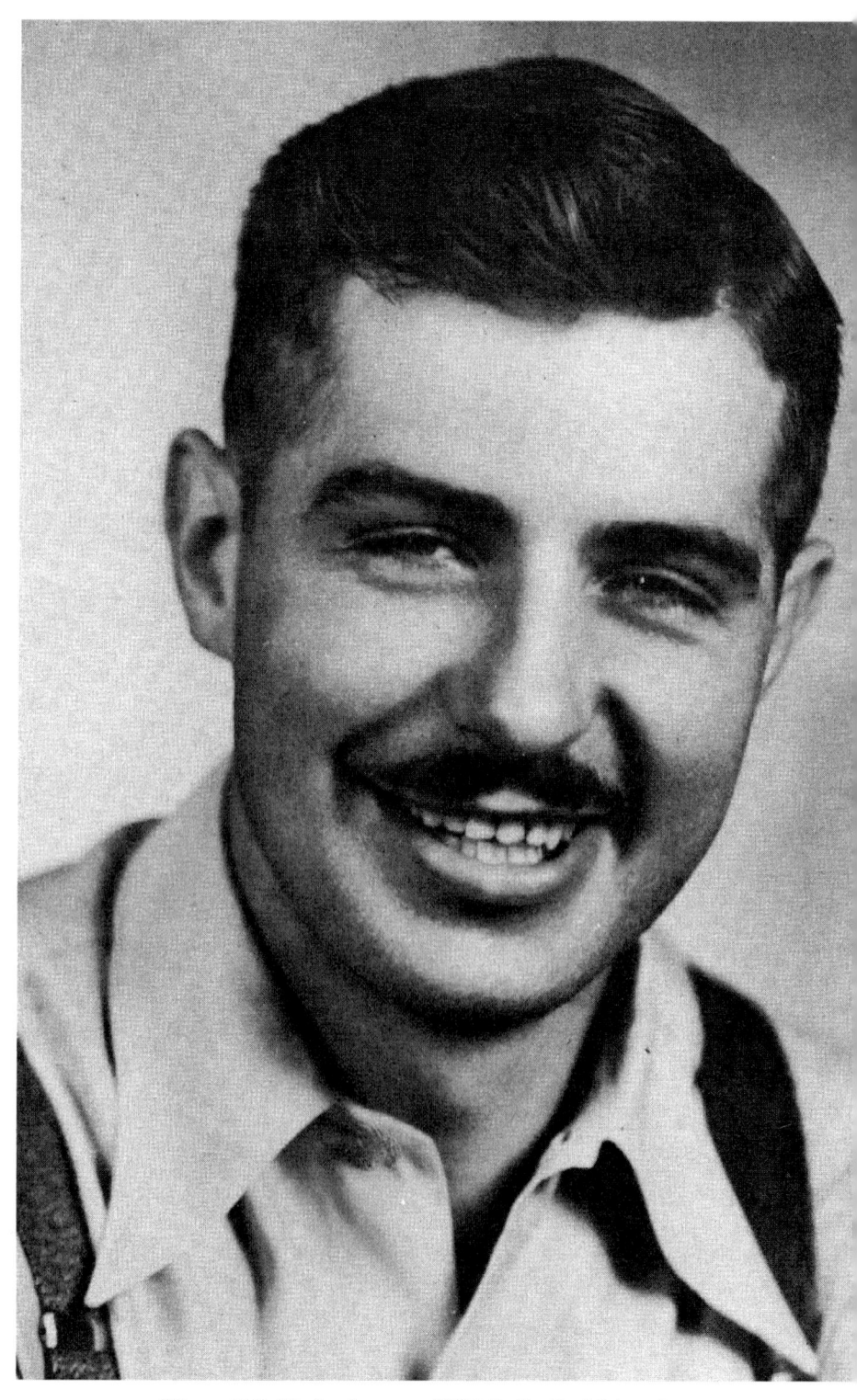

"Happy Al Bell" when he was at WHO-Radio, Des Moines, Iowa.

# Chapter One

My father, Al Bell, was one of those extraordinary persons who could be described as "larger than life." When he roared into a school gymnasium, he was the Orient Express. He filled that gym, packed with school children of every age, with little more than himself, but those kids couldn't take their eyes off Al Bell. He captured them immediately, first by his exotic presence. My dad wore a moustache for most of his life. This factor alone, as simple as it may seem, separated his looks from the average, rural Iowan.

Most of the well-known folks in America who wore moustaches were glamorous movie stars, like Clark Gable, Errol Flynn, David Niven, Dick Powell. The honest truth was that Al Bell looked better in a moustache because of the large space between his nose and upper lip. The cosmetic reasoning, at least in my parents' minds, was that the addition of a moustache gave my dad a more distinctive, even debonair appearance. (Indeed, the only other man in our small town who wore a moustache, was an attractive, successful fellow who was considered a "gentleman farmer.")

Most rural Iowans are descended from European immigrants, with a heavy emphasis on Germanic and Scandinavian backgrounds. Although my dad was an amalgam of British ancestry (Scottish, Irish, English), he defied stereotypes by looking like a glamorous "foreigner." His complexion has been described as "swarthy"; his skin was not particularly dark, but more of an olive tone, similar to Mediterranean races. If you saw his program in September, after he had spent the summer traveling and filming, mowing and haying on his John Deere tractor, with a brief respite of golfing and swimming at the Walther League Camp (now Camp Okoboji), he would indeed be dark, as in deeply tanned. In the Holy Land, Daddy was thought to be an Arab; ironically, my mother was taken for a Jewess. (These assumptions were a great asset in Jerusalem.) In Mexico, especially because of his facility with Spanish, Al Bell was assumed to be a native, as he was in Austria, due to his mastery of the German language.

In sharp contrast to his skin color, my father's eyes were medium light green. As he aged, they became more hazel, mixed with blue and grey, but I remember them to be the green of a farm pond on a stormy day. (My older sister and younger brother have Daddy's green eyes.) With prominent dark eyebrows and long movie star eyelashes, those eyes searched the world and its people for answers. His nose, the "Bell nose" he always called it, was a larger version of my own, a bump halfway down, with a rounded bump on the end, most impressively seen in profile. (My younger brother has a very strong resemblance to our dad.) When you consider that the original Bells from Scotland were descended from Roman invaders, perhaps it makes sense that my dad may have looked Italian.

Daddy's smile was broad and trusting, and he had a very full lower lip. His teeth were crooked, but he never let that stop him from smiling. After all, those were not the days of straight, perfect teeth. But with his wavy brunette hair, combed just so, he was considered quite handsome. In fact, Al Bell was once approached by a Hollywood agent to be drafted as a Clark Gable look-alike for B movies. Daddy said no, thanks.

Secondly, Daddy (and later, Mother) always dressed in the native costumes of the particular country they had visited. To thousands of Iowa schoolchildren who had never been abroad, these costumes lent a surreal flavor to the Al Bell experience. Some costumes were quite elaborate, such as the beautiful Greek outfit of a royal guard, with its crisp, pleated, white skirt, or the black and gold toreador costume from Spain, or the suede lederhosen and jacket from Austria. Daddy inhabited these costumes, and ran out onto the gymnasium floor, shouting a strange greeting in the native tongue of that year's country, Romanian, Morrocan or Navaho. He immediately followed that puzzling outburst with the translation, "Good morning, boys and girls! It's going to be a GRRRRREEEEAAAAT day!"

However, it was not my father's looks or his costumes or his memorable voice that made him larger than life. It was simply the secret of mesmerizing vitality: *joie de vivre,* a joy or passion for life itself. And the kernel of having that quality is Curiosity. Every day of his life, he wanted to know more about everything; sometimes, it was scientific curiosity. When we moved from the city to the farm, he really had to cram. He acquired a vast knowledge of agriculture and animal husbandry between his fulltime job and precious time with family. Fortunately, he sought and listened to his neighbors' advice, and supplemented that with reading "Farm Journal", county extension pamphlets, and other publications.

When Al Bell, the farmer, observed and read about the permanent damage caused by soil erosion, which was primarily caused from plowing rows straight up and down the hills, he began to try new techniques, like plowing rows in a circular fashion around the hills. Black Iowa topsoil was a treasured resource, and he knew it. He

AL BELL tells school youngsters about Don Quixote, a Spanish hero who was immortalized in "Man of LaMancha." A replica of a Spanish ship and other exhibits are shown in the background.

learned that rotating crops was another key to successful planting. One year, a section was planted in corn; the next year it might be oats or soybeans. And when the government told him to let one field go *au naturel,* into alfalfa, for example, he was thrilled to sit back and watch the grass grow.

For a few years, his passion was to study the universe, the solar system, stars. One Christmas, my mother gave Daddy a sizable amateur telescope. That night, he and I tried to ignore the cold chill in our bones, as we checked out the clear skies above our farm. Despite the variables in weather, Daddy would often drag me out when it was barely zero to gaze at the constellation, Orion, with its seven little sisters, the Pleiades. Or on a steamy August night, mosquitoes sucking the blood from our sticky bodies, we would watch for shooting stars, and discuss the ephemeral quality of the Milky Way. Although he, rather than I, was the ambitious student of astronomy books and star maps, he insisted that we learn the skies together. We would venture out for an hour or so most nights, and identify the changing constellations from one season to another. Scorpio, which we could see only partially in the summer, was fascinating with its dragon tail. "The Twins," Gemini and Pollux, among other Greek and Roman-named constellations, motivated lessons in mythology, another of my dad's many interests.

Another phase of Daddy's horticultural studies included raising honey bees. None of us knew then that Al Bell was allergic to bee stings, as he poured himself into learning and working with the industrious, buzzing little insects. The rest of us shied away, literally, from his hobby, but Daddy relished watching his bees gather pollen from the nearby peach trees, learning how they made honey in this miraculous process, and he thoroughly enjoyed eating and sharing honey comb as a sweet treat. I'll never forget, nor did he, as I was the subject of much teasing about it, the first day he brought the bees home in their boxes. I was doing chores, running water at the outside pump at the barn, and suddenly, bees surrounded my face. I froze. "Daddy," I whined softly. He was working setting up the boxes in the orchard, about fifty feet away. "Daddy!" I hissed with exaggerated emphasis on my d's. He still couldn't hear me. I was deathly afraid that if I spoke any louder, I would quickly be devoured by those ferocious bugs. So, in a high, singing voice, I wailed, "Daaaaaaaddy!" I hadn't moved for what seemed like five minutes, and my legs were beginning to tremble.

From the corner of my left eye, I could see my father's head come up, look over at me, and then, he began to laugh. A tear trickled down my right cheek. I hated it when people didn't take me seriously, and yet, being the essential fraidy-cat I was, it occurred frequently. "The BEES!" I spat out through gritted teeth.

"Just tell them to go away," my father chuckled, and he turned back to his work. Tell them to go away? As if they had ears and little brains and knew what I was saying? "Talk gently, but firmly to them, and they'll go away," he added.

So, what did I have to lose? And, I did trust his advice. "Go away," I began tentatively. The bees seemed to stop in flight for a second. I took advantage of this opening to take control of the situation; however, I still had not moved from my paralyzed posture. "You bees just go away now, and leave me alone." Two of them actually drifted away. "Go on now, and get back to what you were doing. I'm busy." I continued bravely. Sure enough, the buzzing faded into the distance, and I was alone again, holding my five gallon bucket. "Whew!" I sat the bucket down and realized that my cramped hand was numb.

"Did it work?" Daddy's voice floated from across the barnyard.

"Yeah. I just told them to go away, and they did just like you said." I felt suddenly strong, proud and confident.

"Well, that's what you have to do whenever you have a problem. Talk to it, and it'll go away." Daddy was right. He was always right until I was fourteen.

There was a period of time shortly after we moved to the farm when our friends from Ames, Clifford and Kitty Hach and their children, Mary and Bruce, visited us fairly often. Cliff was a noted chemist at Iowa State University, and he, like Daddy, yearned to be a Renaissance man. The two friends explored many areas outside of their own expertise, and both respected the other's skills and knowledge in their own fields, as well. When we lived in Ames, Cliff had helped Daddy set up speakers for his record player (in those days, a turntable had become a piece of furniture). My father was eventually bitten by the classical music bug, but only after years of nagging by my mother who had played first chair violin with the Des Moines Symphony. She could barely tolerate the "hillbilly" songs my dad performed at the barn dances and on the radio. He, at the time, judged classical music to be for snooty types who thought they were better than everyone else. It was definitely a bone of contention between them. But, thanks to popular recordings like "The Best of Beethoven," "Mozart's Top Ten," and so on, Al Bell accumulated and enjoyed "long hair" music, much to my mother's relief. Every week after church, as we ate Sunday dinner, we listened to classical music; it became a tradition. More often than not, Al Bell employed music from the masters in his movies.

So, in moving to the farm and building a new house, Daddy needed to set up a new music system. In fact, Cliff had called and waxed enthusiastically about something new called "Hi-Fi." This revolutionary high fidelity sound was done with the use of a "stereo" speaker system. After an afternoon's work of wiring, laughing, sawing and hammering, and more laughing, the two men gave a demonstration to their families. We stood in the middle of the living room, as Daddy put on the album, "Peter and the Wolf" (one of my favorites) by Prokofiev. "Listen to the wolf's theme," Daddy commanded. "It's coming from that speaker above the TV. And Peter's theme is coming from the speaker in the dining room." We all oohed and aahed; we were truly impressed. And then the *piece de resistance*; "Go stand in the bathroom!" This was pure decadence, of course. "For when I'm in the tub," Daddy explained. The proud as punch engineers of modern sound technology had installed speakers all through the house!

On another visit from the Hach family, we all drove down to our local limestone quarry, south on Highway 25 toward Greenfield. My friend, Mary Hach, possessor of a genius IQ, was a Renaissance woman herself at nine years old. (I felt shallow and superficial in comparison.) Mary was currently into fossils. So, the families spread out in the quarry and searched for fossils. I was in awe of this new information. Daddy placed a fossil of a sea shell in the palm of my hand and explained how this quarry had once been an ocean, full of shells. That when the sea dried up, the shell had become embedded, like Plaster of Paris, in the limestone.

Obviously, this insatiable curiosity for finding out what and who resided on the other side of the mountain, lay behind Al Bell's desire to travel. He and my mother traveled all over the world for thirty years, collecting stories, costumes, and artifacts (they referred to these objects as curios). Our house was full of strange and wonderful (and sometimes horrible) mementos: from Kenya, an elephant's foot, I'm sorry to say; a "hubbly bubbly" (an ornate water pipe) from Morocco; a huge tortoise shell from the Galapagos Islands; a shrunken monkey's head from Central America; a beautiful folding screen from Hong Kong; various masks, musical instruments, primitive bowls, vases, and statues, and many more rare findings and peculiar *objets d'art*.

Another requirement for keeping 400 children's attention, was to be worthy of their attention. My dad was a natural entertainer, a "showman." From his first circus production at the age of seven, to his last program (on the Shipibo Indians) at his last church in Arizona, he was at home on the stage. As any performer knows, the very act of giving yourself to an involved audience causes one's adrenalin to increase. That spurt, or in some cases, *explosion*, of energy causes some folks to sweat and shake, but to those who truly desire a pleasurable bond with the audience, we translate that nervous energy into excitement. (On many opening nights, I have advised nervous actors to think "I'm really excited," rather than "I'm really nervous.") Despite many years as a radio

*Al Bell Productions*

## SHIPIBO WORDS

ERO QUA - THANK YOU    HUA = HELLO
MEE AKEE - HOW ARE YOU?
KUSKA IKI = IT'S A GREAT DAY!
BVAH = BOYS    KAVOO = GIRLS
TITI = MAMA    PAPA = PAPA
NIWI RONO = (AL BELL) WIND SNAKE
MUTSA YACA = (RHEA BELL) BEAUTIFUL TO SIT
RUSHEE RONO = (JOHN) STRONG SNAKE
MUHTSA KAHTO = (LOUISE) BEAUTIFUL TO BE AROUND
HANEE = BIG    TAPAN = RAFT
CARA SHAMA = FLAT HEAD
SENAN WEE = TO SPEAK THE TRUTH.
PECKI PECKI = MOTOR BOAT
HATAPA = CHICKEN
PARANTA = BANANAS.
MAHAS = BIG RAT (WE ATE)
IOWASKA = WITCH DOCTOR DRINK

"COWE"
GOOD BYE!

A native Shipibo girl from the jungles of Peru.

announcer and therefore, an unseen performer, Daddy preferred to see his audience, hear their spontaneous reactions, and gauge his level of energy on those reactions.

Al Bell was on stage in one form or another for years before he created Al Bell Productions. He would do almost anything on stage to get laughs, and ultimately, to make money. Several years before I was born, when he was "between engagements" (a euphemism for being out of work), my dad devised a magic show with my mother as his "assistant." My sister saw it and said that everyone was amazed and mystified but her, since she had watched Mother and Daddy practice at home.

Al Bell collected jokes all his life (like Bob Hope and Milton Berle) in a little black book kept in the inside pocket of his suit jacket. He had an appropriate joke for every occasion. He did impersonations of people, both well-known and local characters, complete with funny voices and facial contortions. Farm folks thronged to the barn dances and talent shows he put on all over the state. I wish I had seen one of his most outstanding performances, from the late forties. From what my parents have told me, this is what happened:

> "Happy Al Bell" (his stage name from WHO-Radio, Des Moines) was known for his outrageous surprise openings to these shows, which were attended by hundreds of fans. This particular production took place at the old KRNT Theater in Des Moines. The lights came up as usual at the beginning of the show, but the emcee, Al Bell, was not on the stage. The music started, as a spotlight swept over the auditorium, lighting up the faces of puzzled audience members. Suddenly, from the top balcony, came Daddy's voice, singing, "He flies through the air with the greatest of ease, the daring young man on the flying trapeze!" The spotlight had settled on my dad, balancing on a rail, just before he leapt off the balcony, grasping an actual trapeze that swung him, while he was singing, down, down, down past the hundreds of gasping audience members, until he landed on the stage, to thundering cheers and applause.

Another key to keeping that zest for life? Despite a hard, bitter childhood, Al Bell was an optimist. His favorite anecdote was the classic story of the two little brothers, one an optimist, the other a pessimist, at Christmas. When they came down on Christmas morning to find their presents, the pessimist looked at his myriad gifts spread under the tree, and announced that there weren't enough. The little optimist was told that his gift was in another room. He opened the door to find nothing but fertilizer spread all over the floor. Smiling, he declared, "There's got to be a pony in here somewhere!"

I always wished I could be more optimistic. (My husband Daryl, another hard core optimist, has reformed me since!) Back then, I was influenced more by my mother, who, having learned some hard lessons in her life, became skeptical, and mistrusting. Daddy took pride, however, that my sister Rhea, who was raised when Daddy was much younger and spent more time with my older siblings, had inherited his optimism. He would chide me for not having Rhea's attitude. "Keep digging, Becky. There's a pony in there somewhere!"

My dad also possessed the double weapons of charm and charisma. He had learned how to be charming as a little boy. Al Bell wanted to be liked, and, at an early age, he figured out how. "My, what a pretty red dress you have on," he might have said to his eight year-old girlfriend, as he certainly would have said it to an eighty year-old grandmother. He practiced this charm all his life, until it was as natural for him to say to a complete stranger, "Wow! You know so much about fishing that I could listen to you for hours," as it was to tell one of my friends, "Curly, you have the most gorgeous naturally curly hair I've ever seen, except of course, for my wife, and your hair looks a lot like hers!"

Charm is, unfortunately, a double-edged sword. Most of the time, Al Bell was an expert at knowing how far to go, how far to stretch the truth, how long to keep oozing that magnetic goo all over his subjects. For the most part, he really was sincere. But in my dad's reality, he had to sell not only his programs, but himself. He always told us, "You can catch more flies with honey than with vinegar." My mother, who preferred the blunt truth to charming lies, would scold my dad at times for "pouring it on too thick." And yet, she knew that only Al Bell could win over grumpy superintendents, indecisive principals, and resistant audiences with his type of old-fashioned charm. Again, he really liked most people, and most of these school administrators became good friends over the thirty years that he did business with them.

Charisma is another matter. According to *The New York Times Everyday Reader's Dictionary of Misunderstood, Misused, Mispronounced Words,* charisma is "an outstanding quality in a person that gives him influence and authority over others." Experience certainly gives us influence and authority, but what is that magic quality in charisma that separates the amateurs from the pros? *Webster's New International Dictionary* defines charisma as "having a divine or spiritual gift," I believe that the Lord is responsible for that special spark placed within each of us, but when it comes to charisma, did He give it to every seventeenth or seventieth person? Or is it genetic? My dad's family was not especially dynamic. Or is this a gift that can be cultivated?

I'd like to think of charisma as a quality, innate or learned, that is based on an enthusiasm for life, which brings us back to *joie de vivre*. However you define it, charisma is that quality that draws us, inexorably, to certain people, and yet, requires that we remain in awe of said special person. We want to be close to a charismatic individual, not just because some of that magic may rub off on us, but because the person with charisma is electric, magnetic, even hypnotic. Life is more exciting for these unique human beings, and we are lifted from our hum-drum, normal lives when we are in their presence. The title character in "The Rainmaker" by N. Richard Nash , was a charismatic outcast, as was Sinclair Lewis' "Elmer Gantry," a powerful preacher. (Both of these roles were beautifully and tragically portrayed by Burt Lancaster, who used to remind me of my father.) In Neil Simon's, "The Goodbye Girl," the character of Eliot Garfield is described as having charisma. Richard Dreyfuss who played Eliot in the movie, won a Best Actor Oscar for his performance. I admit he's a fine actor, but is it not the role of Eliot, written by the screenwriter, who deserves the applause? And, perhaps, this quality is the elusive and nameless "It" that Hollywood actors strive for. My favorite actress, Katharine Hepburn, was quoted as saying, "Whatever It is, I've got it!" Without a doubt, my father had It. Perhaps, I should say that he had charisma when he was "on." My dad, like all actors, could turn it on or off. At home, he could be very funny or entertaining or even dramatic, but given an audience, the man became golden.

Returning to my first premise, that Al Bell was "larger than life," I must admit that much of the skill here is in that tried and true method of hyperbole: exaggeration. The terrifying headhunter, who

Daddy captured on film in "Sons of Shipibo," doesn't appear quite as frightening onscreen as when Al Bell described him in person in his lecture. The wild tribal witchdoctor, who my dad impersonated before the Shipibo movie, looks rather ordinary, standing among the other natives for a group photo. Through dramatic and humorous exaggeration, my dad conjured up more colorful images than dry reality may have revealed. Exaggeration, like charm, must be handled cautiously, however. In my dad's mind, an adjective like *spooky*, became much more powerful when preceded with *horrifyingly* or, at least, *very*. And if *very* wasn't strong enough, you just had to add another one, as in *very, very spooky*.

Al Bell's gift for story telling was certainly enhanced with his flair for comedy and drama, his gift for impersonation, his animated expressions, and a penchant for exaggeration. However, he never stopped growing and "honing his craft," as actors put it. In college and his early married life, he planted and harvested a daily crop of vocabulary words by attaching a new word every morning to a clothes line tied across one corner of the room. For example, "Today's word is prestidigitator" (magician). He would see it, spell it, and sprinkle his conversation with it. Daddy had an extensive vocabulary, and he used it not to impress, but to articulate exactly what he meant to say.

Daddy practiced telling his jokes in the car, where he spent most of his time, traveling from one school to another (he generally did four shows a day, if the towns were close enough together). But he knew he needed an audience to test every joke, so when he came home, we kids and Mother would be his test audience. Often he would instruct us, "Now, I could have waited longer to say the punch line, but if you do that, then your listener starts to laugh, and they miss the really funny word at the end. That happened the first time I told it. But if you wait just long enough, so they've heard the important clue word, but not long enough for them to think about it, they'll laugh their heads off." Timing was a practiced skill, as was inflection. We would hear him saying a word one way and then another, to see which was funnier. Of course, as all comedians know, there are just some naturally funny words. *Chicken*, for example. It must be placed in a certain position in the sentence for maximum effect. When it came to joke telling, we Bell kids learned at the feet of the master. He had a great sense of humor himself, and he worked on his material until it was foolproof. "Now, they'll laugh here and here, and then I'll get 'em real quiet with this next story, and when they hear about the snakes, all the girls will scream." And they did.

My dad, like most other story and joke tellers, was not above "borrowing" styles or material. In the evening, we all watched television, and Daddy gleaned from his favorite comedians what he considered to be the best or most popular styles of the time. Therefore, he went through a period of telling his jokes in a simple, naive fashion, like George Gobel. Daddy was also a big fan of the blustery character, Ralph Kramden, created by Jackie Gleason on the "Honeymooners." His voice and mannerisms became overly boisterous and rough. "To the moon, Alice, to the moon!" Perhaps his very favorite funny man was the gentle and giggly Red Skelton. During his Red Skelton phase, Al Bell would laugh as he told the joke, in anticipation of the punch line. This was in direct violation of his "never laugh at your own joke" rule, but it seemed to work for him, as listeners chuckled along with him before he ever delivered the punch line. "If you let them know how funny it is in advance, they warm up for it and get ready to laugh."

It was a huge triumph to get our dad to laugh at one of our jokes. My gregarious sister became the best joke teller among us kids. She, like Daddy, gladly played the fool, in order to get the big laugh at the end. (I tried, but failed repeatedly, due to my fear of embarrassing myself.) Of course, there was the time when I was in high school, preparing for an upcoming speech contest, that my dad really surprised me. My mother was the family speech coach. She had taken several speech classes in her day, beginning with what was called "elocution." By the time she entered college, she had performed readings, solos, any and everything a public speaker needs to be confident. But her manner of speaking, which seemed affected to many folks, made her stand out in our little community. Emphasis on articulation, especially "crisp" consonants and pure vowels, pitch, inflection, and so on, were her specialty. My friends always asked, "Why does your mother talk like that?" It was embarrassing at times, like at ball games, to hear my mother over-pronounce familiar phrases, like "Get in there and fight!" Each *t* and *d* and *f* was exaggerated, so that it seemed she might be yelling to a deaf person, rather than at her son playing football.

Nevertheless (one of my mother's favorite words), she had trained me night after night on my humorous monologue, "The Darling Little Trailer." Much to my chagrin, I couldn't just stand and recite it. Please! I was fourteen, and very self-conscious. My arms were glued to the side of my body, and Mother had to yank them away, so they would be free to gesture. "Louder!" she would yell at me. "Your eyes, let's see them pop open!" She was relentless, and a much better coach than I ever gave her credit for. Finally, on a wintry Friday night (Daddy came home every Friday night after a hectic week of up to twenty programs), Mother made him sit in the kitchen and listen to my now polished piece. I popped my eyes, I was loud, I was animated, but my father never changed his expression. "Boy, he's more critical than Mother," I thought as I slyly stole a peek at him. I worked as hard as I could, mimicking my mother's expressions. The climax to my funny story was coming, and my dad hadn't even cracked a smile! "Okay! So you're the professional!" I thought resentfully. I was about to give up, but staggered to the end. Silence. My mother applauded, and told me I'd done a good job, and I should do well in the contest the following day. My dad finally spoke up, slowly, and looked at me penetratingly.

"I didn't know our little girl had a lisp."

A what?! Surely, I'd been transported to another planet and was ensnared by giant spiders. I couldn't talk, I couldn't respond. I was in shock. A lisp? Luckily, my mother broke in to chide him for making a big deal out of something that didn't matter right then, but I had to leave the room. "Thanks, Dad," I whispered to myself, as I sought refuge in my teenage sanctuary to contemplate this new revelation. I had a speech impediment!

My mother was, and had been, an excellent teacher. My dad, as teacher, fared better with people in large crowds. The more the better, because that meant he could stay in his stage persona, and wouldn't have to be concerned with relationships and other people's feelings. In his path to become a successful entertainer and lecturer, it was necessary for him to develop tunnelvision. Although most folks assumed that his business was a one-man show, that was hardly the case. He couldn't have kept it all together without my mother's organizational and research skills. Few people knew that she worked as Daddy's secretary every day at home, writing letters, sending out flyers, calling schools to schedule programs, etc. However, it **appeared** to be all Daddy, and it's true that before she joined him on the road (per his doctor's orders), Al Bell answered only to himself five days a week.

Because he had almost always been a one-man show, Daddy

focused intensely on himself. Obviously, this resulted in a fairly self-centered personage who was away from home a lot. He worked incredibly hard every week, and he would be exhausted by the time he arrived home on Friday nights. Too often, we kids became needy for his attention, and he frequently responded abruptly, as in "Let's go see your room. Did you clean it this week? I want to see beds made, at least!" If we'd had a long week at school, too, and our rooms were a mess, Daddy would lose his temper or say something sarcastic. I confess that I was the big baby in the family; I often cried when he confronted me with the unvarnished truth. "Your room looks like a pig sty!" he yelled at me once. And it did. In retrospect, this was a man who was genuinely fatigued from hours and hours of driving all over Iowa, after too many quick trips under pressure on short-cut gravel roads. By Friday, his voice was almost always hoarse from constant use, day in and day out.

Quite often, when I met new friends like at camp, kids would whisper, "She's Al Bell's daughter!" to each other, and I had to be prepared for the next shoe to drop. "What's he like at home?" (All of us Bell kids had to deal with this; it was a source of pride on one hand, but uncomfortable on the other, trying not to seem like a show-off or snob.) In time, I was able to discern what to tell and what not to, because personal details had no place in these conversations! Usually, I'd say that he was funny, because he was. He was easy and affectionate with me, but this had more to do with my being the "planned" child out of the bunch. I was "Daddy's girl" for most of my life, which was a blessing and a curse, or "blurse," as my husband puts it. Al Bell became very impatient with all of us at times, but I got off more easily than the others which was obvious to everyone, especially my siblings.

For nine months out of the year, except for weekends and holidays, Al Bell belonged to the school kids of Iowa. Yes, he signed a lot of autographs and received a lot of fan mail. On arriving at a typical school, he would have young boys help him carry his equipment: a large movie screen and tripod stand that rolled and folded up into a long shiny blue tube; his sixteen millimeter projector, wrapped inside a case or quilted cover (custom made by Mother); a speaker and amplifier for his sound system, a suitcase full of curios, a suitcase full of costume and accessories, plus, quite frequently, a live animal. (More on that later.) Daddy carried the bulkiest and heaviest items, while a cadre of boys fought over who got to carry whatever he'd let them grab. He was a hero to these boys. My dad had figured out early on, that he would have to dispense with learning all the boys' names at every school, so he called the first and boldest kid, "George." Every school had a young volunteer named George. I remember once when I commented on this practice, he added the fact that sometimes a young man would proudly announce, "I was George last year. Can I be George again?"

Al Bell thrived on the road and in the schools. He really did enjoy giving the programs, especially to the younger kids in the audience. They were more easily entertained, and his brand of corn fit them to a proverbial T. He worked extremely hard to address the high schoolers, to keep their attention. Most of the smaller schools gathered the entire school, kindergarten through twelfth grade, into one gym or auditorium for one show. (Often, there were as many as 500 big and little children, plus most of the teachers, an administrator or two if they could make it, and a few visiting parents or alumni.) Teenagers, in the midst of their angst and insecurities, often made catcalls or called out supposedly funny remarks to my dad, and for the most part, Daddy was used to it and had prepared appropriate quips to settle them down. In later years, however, as teens evolved to become a seemingly fearless entity, lacking respect for any authority, they could disrupt that magic ambience that my dad strove to attain for every show. That's why Al Bell's challenge was monumental—in my opinion, anyway. How to keep the attention of the older kids while catering to the little ones, and vice versa. It was a science. He had stories and jokes for each age group, mixed and blended and timed, so that, hopefully, the whole group would stay as mesmerized as his core fans were.

"How did your dad get into this business, anyway?" many people asked. Quite simply, he created it. "But how did he think of it?" Because of "conflicts with management" at dozens of jobs over the years, my dad realized that he had to become his own boss. Sure, there were other assembly programs out there—several in fact, in the early years. Programs similar to Al Bell's were called travelogues. Most of them were BOR-ING! Daddy's genius was that he took what he loved doing: entertaining and photography, and, combined them with what he wanted to do—to see the world. Because of this love, this life-long curiosity and passion for life, no one could hold a candle to his unique style of assembly programs. A twenty minute lecture before the movie, and then the movie had to be no more than twenty-eight minutes long. Those precious leftover minutes were left for setting up, changing into his costume, and tearing down. One hour. No more, no less. For a dime. Or maybe a quarter. In some schools, kids didn't have to bring change in their pockets on Al Bell Day; the school board or the PTA or some connected organization paid for it.

After twenty years, my mother gave my father an ultimatum: raise your prices. There was no "or else." Daddy argued and worried. "They'll stop inviting me to come! Last week, Mr. Smith (or Jones) told me that they've had to cut out all their other assembly programs." For a man with a big ego, he had minimal self-confidence about his staying power.

"Allen." My mother would remain patient for the first, maybe two minutes. " I am on the phone every day with these administrators. They **love** you. If one or two cancel, that's fine. I have five schools now that are on the waiting list for cancellations."

"But I don't want to be the highest paid program out there," he would counter.

"Why not? We spend more on our trips and costumes and curios and quality of film processing..."

"But, it just won't look good when I show up. They'll make comments like, 'Upping your price, huh, Al? You and the wife going to the moon next year?'"

"Allen! We've been charging the same fee for twenty years! Look through the bills from last summer. And you've been whining over that old projector. What if it breaks down again, and you can't show the movie at all?"

"Oh, all right...But I don't like it, and neither will they," he would protest.

"Let me deal with them on the phone. (Good cop, bad cop?) I'll tell them what airplane fare has gone up to since last year." My mother had logic on her side.

Finally, after much bickering and badgering, Daddy would give in. Mother would advise the superintendents and principals that the price for an Al Bell program had just gone up to fifty dollars. No one balked. Oh, maybe one, but he'd been a poop, anyway.

Larger than life. Charisma. Charm. Curiosity. Love. Zest. Enthusiasm. Electricity. Mesmerizing. Entertainer. Teacher. Actor. Musician. My dad. Al Bell.

# Chapter Two

My dad was born with a hole in his heart. Actually two, but not being a medical person, I will simplify his condition, so that the layperson can understand. In truth, I fear getting more technical will expose my own ignorance on the subject. My parents talked about my dad's heart so often, that I'm sure I must have comprehended and remembered all the terms, fifty years ago, but as Thomas Edison said, "My mind is like a set of drawers, and when one gets too full, I empty it out!" The terms were not pertinent to my adult life, so "Left ventricle, right auricle," were tossed out of my memory drawer. The bottom line is that Daddy's hole(s) prevented the new, circulated and oxygenated blood from refreshing my father's heart. He ran on tired blood that had already been around and through his body. It is not important to know all the terms; suffice it to say that Al Bell's health was compromised at birth, and most babies with this condition would not have survived before the age of respirators, defibrillators, and so on.

We do know that doctors predicted that Daddy would not live past the age of seven. The next time that medical examinations were done, the doctors predicted that he would not live past the age of twenty-one. Enter my mother. Al Bell thought it only fair that his first serious girlfriend should be informed as to his temporal state of affairs. My mother, being the worrier that she was, took this news very seriously. Unbeknownst to my dad, she became his caregiver when they were in college. After every date, that is, after Al Bell delivered Rhea Morgan to the door of her musical sorority house, she would wait a few minutes, and then surreptitiously, follow *him* home! Thus began a lifelong quality to their relationship: being a traditional male of that era, he believed that he was the Protector; she alone knew that her beau's life depended on necessary precautions, and she provided them.

Naturally, my mother divulged this information to her husband at some point, probably when he pushed her too far on an issue, and she finally showed her cards. "One- upmanship" is not recommended for marriage; however, I have no doubt that it happens frequently. This role as my dad's permanent caregiver changed my mother. She became a chronic worrier, and somewhat of a doomsayer. Every day that Al Bell lived meant that my mom was one day closer to losing him forever. The freedom to breathe, which marriage gives most spouses, so that they can settle into secure normalcy, was not available to Rhea Bell. The families of cancer patients are very familiar with this state of mind. The advice to "live one day at a time" is not only practical, but mentally healthy; however, it is easier said than done.

My parents had a ritual that began with Daddy's confession, "I don't feel so good." Mother would put her head on his chest and listen to the irregular heartbeats. "It's going buh-Dum, dum, budda Dum dum," she would report.

"I can feel it," my dad would affirm. Fortunately, with the advance of home medical devices such as stethoscopes, my parents' growing knowledge of my dad's condition led to a more casual attitude. "I think I'll just lie down for awhile," he would say.

"Good idea," my mother would respond. "I'll call you when dinner's ready."

As a result of his heart condition, my dad suffered chronic fatigue, but we kids were rarely aware of it. And I'm sure that thousands of Iowa schoolchildren had no idea that this powerful icon had any kind of health problems. The pulsing life force in my dad's makeup dominated his purposeful life. When he returned home after an intense week of driving and entertaining, he may have settled into his big green chair to watch TV with us, but the next day, we would find him out mending fences (a never ending chore,) or shelling corn, killing chickens, or fixing the plumbing . He loved his life on the farm. It was often labor-intensive, but it was also distracting, simple, and comfortable, compared with being on the road. Salesmen who disappear with a fishing pole on weekends can relate.

It's amazing that Al Bell was athletic at all, but he was. As an avid golfer, a powerful swimmer, and a daily weight lifter (lifting heavy equipment in and out of the car and up and down school stairs), my dad was in better shape than the "average bear." Rhea and Allen, my siblings, who are a few years older than I, remember their father as a competitive athlete who used to walk on his hands across the lawn. Daddy was an acrobat/gymnast, as well, when he was in his twenties and thirties. His body was flexible, his muscles supple. He taught his first two kids how to do cartwheels, tumbling, and even back flips.

But I remember clearly that my dad was always subject to dizziness and fainting when he reached elevated heights. His worst episode occurred when the Bells were filming in Machu Picchu, Peru. At seventeen thousand feet above sea level, Daddy's heart quit working, and he went into heart failure. A witch doctor was sent for by the locals, but Mother and Daddy knew that their smartest option was to pray, and pray hard. They both attested to the miracle that followed hours of fervent prayer; the witch doctor, who danced a few steps and uttered mumbo-jumbo, was thanked and dismissed early on in the evening.

The harsh reality of my dad's cigarette habit eventually took its toll when my brother Doug and I were growing up. Daddy developed sinus problems, a nagging cough, and shortness of breath when climbing stairs, lifting heavy loads and walking long distances. As all teachers know, Al Bell was exposed to zillions of germs at every school. Kids would rush up to him after the program to shake his hand and ask last-minute questions. As a result, Daddy caught colds and the flu more easily. He rarely stayed home to recover, however, since his work ethic was such that he couldn't let down "his kids" in the schools, besides, every program meant another twenty-five dollars to pay for a constantly hungry gas tank.

About my sophomore year in high school, I became aware that Daddy and Mother were discussing the possibility of heart surgery for my father. The first requirement for Al Bell, however, was to quit smoking. For anyone who has tried to or actually quit smoking, you have felt addiction at its ugliest. You know the intense cravings and ongoing temptation to cheat. If quitting had been easy, of course, my father would have done it years before. But his doctors made it clear that his future was tentative without closing that ever-widening hole in his heart, and cigarettes absolutely could not be a part of my dad's future. In fact, he had to quit smoking for six months before the operation would even be scheduled. I confess that I, too, was an addict to cigarettes at one time, and I know how daunting this deadline was to my dad. A friend suggested that Daddy buy lemon drops to keep his mouth occupied, so he did. Whenever we rode in the car, he would offer everyone else a lemon drop. These were sugar and corn syrup lemon drops; there were no sugar-free alternatives in those days. The lemon drops disappeared quickly and even bothered his tongue after awhile, so Daddy changed to cherry. Yum! If Doug and I were in the car, we always had a cherry drop in our mouths. Al Bell's temptation to smoke was gradually ebbing away, because he was now addicted to hard candy! We kids approved of the butterscotch treats, too, so one day, when we reached into the little white bag next to his car seat, we pulled out what smelled to be poison! We tried one. We were addicted by now, too, and quickly spit out *horehound* drops. Yuck! "How come you changed to these icky ones, Daddy?"

"You kids were eating so many that I realized I was spending too much money. I figured you wouldn't like the horehound flavor, and I see that I was right!"

Plans gradually came together for my parents to travel to Minneapolis for **one of the first ever open-heart surgeries**. Somewhere, on some medical library shelf, Al Bell's case is written up as an early case history. This was 1963. Mother worried, of course, that he might not make it through the operation (he was given a fifty percent chance of surviving), but Daddy, the optimist, kept raving about the excellent reputation and track record that his doctors had earned. I was old enough to take care of my younger brother and the farm chores, and Mother called every night while they were gone. When they returned, we kids adapted to a regimen that called for absolute quiet while our dad rested, and taking over extra chores and errands to minimize our mom's already busy schedule. She was swamped with re-scheduling school programs, of course. Most administrators were very sympathetic, but some irritatingly stolid folks whose school calendars were carved in stone, kvetched and moaned. Much to my parents' frustration, a few cancelled the program altogether that year.

My dad's resilience was astounding. With a few admonitions from his doctors, and many more from my mother, Al Bell went back on the road. It wasn't long before we fell back into established patterns and habits. It didn't occur to me at the time, but one of my dad's biggest triumphs was the fact that he never smoked again. The doctors had given him a loophole after surgery, possibly from downright begging on my father's part, but bless his heart, he realized that once he had quit, he had to stop smoking forever. Daddy had always been a wiry, slim workaholic, but now he began to enjoy life at a slower pace. Food tasted better, and with time, he put on weight. By the 1970s, Al Bell was almost chunky.

It was Christmas of 1968 when my best friend Patty Jo and I spent our hard-earned money to fly to New York City to see as many Broadway shows as we could pack into our five-day adventure. I called home on New Year's Eve, our last night in the Big Apple, to exchange salutations with my parents. They had been dancing at the Greenfield Country Club that night and were still awake and merry. As Patty Jo and I boarded our flight home, melodies and scenes of Pearl Bailey and Cab Calloway in "Hello, Dolly" danced in our heads. Lines from "Man of La Mancha" and "Mame" floated through our conversation. However, when we landed in Des Moines, all gaiety stopped. I was told by a stewardess that my dad was in Mercy Hospital in Des Moines, and I was to call this number and talk to my mom. Shaking, I dialed the number. Mother tried to be calm and reassuring. Daddy had suffered a stroke. I knew I must be strong for my mother. But as the taxi carried us girls to the hospital, challenging questions shook my universe. How could Al Bell possibly carry on his programs if he had suffered a paralyzing stroke? What would my mother do? What if, God forbid, he died? It was impossible to imagine.

My dad's speech had already been partially repaired through his own diligent work. Mother was so proud of him. I was stunned, of course, to hear my father speak with a hesitating lisp, but I had to appreciate what my mom was telling me. It had been really scary for both of them when they first noticed that his mouth was paralyzed on one side. "We may have to reschedule a few programs, but Daddy's going to be just fine!" she assured me.

Daddy nodded, and with great difficulty, added, "The Lord wants me to live and continue to do my programs. Don't worry. I'm fine."

Observing my dad's determination versus his demanding career, the doctors now set up harsh restrictions on Al Bell. "Retire now, or take your wife with you on the road. She must make sure that you do not overdo, that you do not carry your own equipment..." It was a terribly traumatic time for my mother. Traveling with my father meant leaving my brother, then a senior in high school, at home by himself all week. Daddy's schedule was up to almost five hundred schools by now; he couldn't disappoint all those kids. And with the financial responsibility of his family's future on his head, Al Bell was hell-bent on continuing the programs. With a heavy heart, Mother went on the road with Daddy, taking over half of the lecture, carrying equipment, and sharply reprimanding those students or principals who gave Al Bell a hard time. Her heart was broken, however, over the two males who wanted her attention. Because she had to assert herself and take over all the business and the inevitable conflicts, along with keeping her husband on an even keel, she found herself on the phone at every available time, talking to my brother, cheering him on with his wrestling, and trying to support him long distance. Another crisis to digest and work through.

Daddy's life had been and would continue to be a great experimental journey through wide rivers of professional success and narrow canyons of health crises. It was in December of 1977 that Mother and Daddy fought their way through a terrible blizzard on their way home from their last program. They were in southeastern Iowa, many hours from home, and Al Bell did something he'd never done. He asked my mother to drive. He felt too bad, he said, to go on. So, Mother, who had been driving since she borrowed a car at the age of fourteen, took over. The blizzard was unforgiving. Neither wanted to stop to take refuge. Mother was probably reminding Daddy that William Douglas Bell was waiting for them at home; they had promised to be home in time for a wrestling tournament, followed by an evening out at a nice restaurant. Daddy merely wanted to sleep in his own bed. Never had he felt so exhausted. Never had he wanted so badly to be off these miserably icy roads. Mother was driving with great difficulty, and talking her way through it. "I can't tell if that's the edge of the road or the edge of the snowdrift," she would say. "Oh, Daddy, you're so good at getting home in this kind of weather. Can't you please take it the rest of the way?" With his dear companion, the Lord, on his side, Al Bell took over the wheel again. For two more hours, they bucked snow drifts until they got on Interstate 80, and finally arrived in Des Moines. But my dad could not continue driving. He was, and had been experiencing heart failure. He drove directly to the hospital. Mother called Doug, of course, and then me. My mother sobbed on the phone.

I arrived at the hospital shortly after they did. My Dad's heart was in trouble. After too long a time waiting, Daddy, Mother and I were told the verdict: a pacemaker. Hello? A what? Thank God for

Daddy and I at Christmas, 1982 in Arizona.

the doctors who invented the pacemaker. Daddy went through two of them in his last years.

After my parents retired to Tucson, Arizona, they were both periodically in and out of the University of Arizona Hospital, a research hospital. Al and Rhea Bell were well known to their doctors and nurses alike. My mother had a rare condition that resulted in very sudden, very high blood pressure. Daddy's heart history amazed and fascinated the experts. When my dad's body finally succumbed after a full and active life, the doctors asked if they could do an autopsy on Al Bell. "Of course!" my mother cried. "**Please** do an autopsy!" Maybe they would find out exactly how he lived so long. Seventy-seven years! But she was totally taken by surprise, when the doctor came and asked, "What would you think if you donated his eyes, for example, to science?" My mother was nonplussed. Daddy had gone through cataract surgery just a couple years prior to his death. That didn't matter, they said. "What about his other organs?" they asked.

"If there is any part of my husband's body that can help someone or help the University of Arizona to understand more about science, then, by all means, do it!" she cried.

I was so proud of her. Amazingly enough, Al Bell's eyes were used for a transplant within just a few hours. "Just think," my mother conjectured, with tears in her eyes, "Someone will be able to see because of Daddy! It would have made him so happy."

## Chapter Three

We moved to the farm from Ames in the early summer of 1953. I had just finished the first grade, but we were several days late in arriving, due to my being hospitalized with a kidney infection. Herb Cunningham, Menlo farmer, had been a big fan of Daddy's when "Happy Al Bell" was popular on WHO-Radio. After meeting at some event, Herb and Daddy became long-distance buddies. Al Bell Productions had become a reality (and was no longer being done on a proverbial shoestring), but whenever we visited w/Herb and his family, my dad looked longingly at country life. Daddy really wanted out of the city and out of the radio station business. So, Herb Cunningham told Al Bell about the small farm directly across the road. They walked over and looked at the falling down old house. Herb took Daddy on his tractor and they looked over the eighty acres. My father was seriously planning a move; however, my mother, just as seriously, objected.

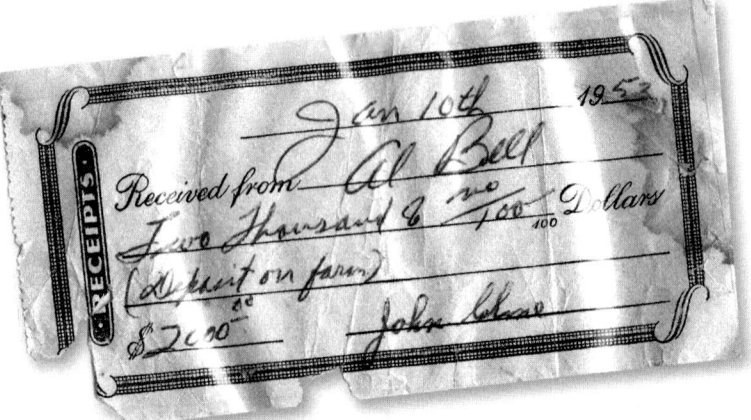

Receipt from the deposit on the Menlo farm, 1953.

Not that she wasn't a hard worker; Rhea Bell did chores, drove the tractor when needed, threw bales of hay down to the cows in the barn, and after each blizzard, shoveled out our long driveway like a trooper. But she was a born and bred city girl, and Mother could see the big picture: Al Bell would leave her five days a week to pursue his new career, and she would be stranded fifty miles from Des Moines, the closest cultural center. After all, my mother was a trained musician, and she thrived on attending concerts and hosting bridge clubs. She did NOT want to live "way out in the country." My dad was adamant. And she paid the price for it. All seventeen years she lived on the farm, Mother longed for the day she could return to the city. But Daddy and we four kids loved the farm.

Because Menlo was too far to commute from Ames in those days, my parents accepted Herb's offer to live in the Cunningham garage while we tore down the old house, and built a new one. It was probably 12 x 20 with one door, the big sliding garage door. God bless the Cunninghams! They shared their outhouse with us as well.

First, we had to tear down the house on our new property. The old, boxy two-story house was falling apart, literally. My job was to carry out lath after Daddy and Allen pried it off the walls. My dad would hammer at the old plaster (which lay behind several layers of wallpaper), and then, using the claws of the hammer, or a pry bar, pull hunks of wall into the room. It was a terribly dirty job, accompanied by clouds of plaster dust. Rhea divided her time between working with Mother, who shoveled piles of ancient plaster, nails and garbage into the center of the room, and keeping track of her little brother who not only got into everything, but occasionally disappeared. I remember lots of wasp nests and hornets, zooming around our heads, plenty angry for having their nests exposed and ripped apart. Occasionally, Daddy's tool struck through hollow walls or disintegrating flooring, and down it would come – an avalanche of lung-choking junk.

The plan Mother and Daddy had worked out was to tear down the house as quickly as possible, saving only the best of the old wood. After digging out a bigger basement and laying a concrete foundation, Daddy brought in Jake Schwartzkopf, a carpenter of local renown, who framed the new house. Meanwhile, work was going on in the basement, so we could move in before winter hit.

Our basement home was quite cozy for the next year: cool in the summer, and not too terrible during the winter. We all slept in one room, and it was tight! (This room later became our fall-out shelter during the Cold War.) We had a large living area, directly below where our new living room was being designed. The tiny bathroom was freezing in January, but we had installed a shower, so if you turned it on hot for a minute, the steam warmed the area enough to disrobe.

When Daddy and Mother described the future plans for our house upstairs, it sounded "better than

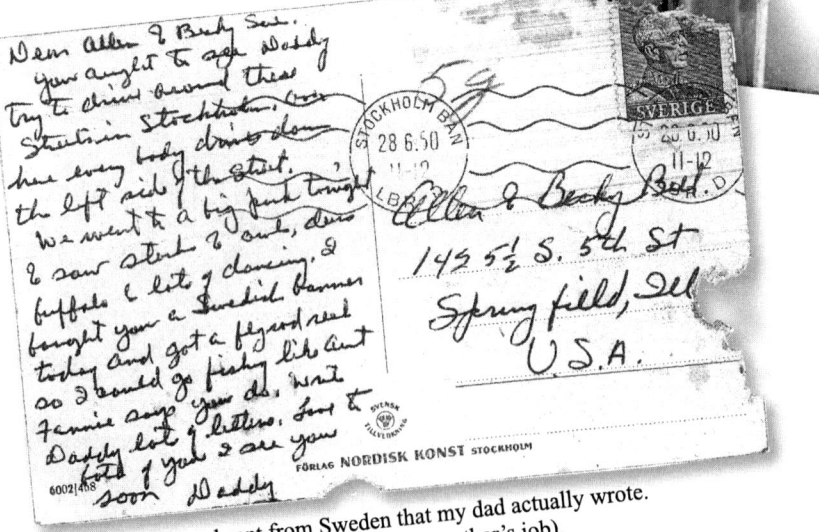

A postcard sent from Sweden that my dad actually wrote. (It was considered to be mother's job).

Walt Disney's house" to me. (What did I know about Mr. Disney's house?) Every night, regardless of what was on TV downstairs, we worked upstairs, sanding our new shelves and sliding doors. I hate sanding. People who enjoy this activity are inordinately strange. But our parents had grown up in the twenties and thirties. The work ethic reigned. "Sanding is good for your character." Mother worked endlessly sewing curtains, bedspreads and matching pillow covers, not to mention making clothes for my sister and me. We all helped to put up wallpaper in the kitchen and lay linoleum in the kitchen and bathroom. Every time I displayed a whiney attitude, my parents reminded me how my bedroom would look someday. Eventually, I realized how hard they had been working, and respected their unflagging tenacity.

The old well outside exuded history and authenticity. More importantly, we drank well water from that old well for many years. It was refreshingly cold, crisp, and clean tasting. The well was deep, and the pump platform stood in the front yard near the driveway. I remember that the pump handle squeaked noisily as I worked it up and down. This great water, tasty as it was, contained gobs of iron. A few years later, my parents concluded that this basically rusty water was not so great. Rust stains decorated the sinks, the sheets, the towels, my mother's best white blouse.

We carried water from that well for the first couple years. Buckets were placed on the gas stove and boiled, so we could have hot water. Because this was so labor intensive, we all shared basically the same bathwater. Daddy got the first bath, because he could stand the hottest water. I'm not sure who went next, but whoever wasn't in the tub, got to carry another bucket of hot water in to keep the water temperature stable. My turn was near the end; by this time, soap suds had turned into a gray sludge which clung to the edges of the tub. Doug was last; luckily, he was too little to be very discriminating.

As in all things, with time and plenty of labor, the place came together. The house was still a work in progress when we moved upstairs, so Al Bell's weekends at home were hectic. Daddy's plan for the living room fireplace involved hauling in large rocks from the fields. I remember him fitting the rocks together like a puzzle around the fireplace opening. It was a work of art. We all loved our fireplace and purchased fire tools for Daddy on one of our first Christmases there. (During blizzards, when the power went out, we were very grateful for the fireplace!) Our living room was open into the dining room, and with picture windows on each side, it felt like a huge, freeing space.

The Bell house was one of the first ranch-style houses in the area. It seemed so big back then, but when I came back many years later, I could tell that I had had the perspective of a little girl.

Rhea and I shared a bedroom, so did Allen and Doug. I loved to go into their room with the knotty pine walls and bunk beds; it felt like Camp Okoboji. Mother and Daddy's room was larger, with Mother's hand sewn rose-patterned bedspread and matching curtains. Her sewing machine was always busy in those days. Mother had requested a cedar closet for linens and some storage. It smelled so yummy that sometimes I'd go in, shut the door and inhale that earthy aroma in the dark. The kitchen was decorated with bright yellow curtains which were made from fiberglass, something new. I couldn't comprehend this information; why didn't they break when they were washed? I asked Mother. The linoleum squares were placed in a neat yellow and brown checkerboard pattern, and Daddy carved out a bell shape in the center square. Folks around Menlo drove by our pretty ranch house with the big mowed yard, the white fence lining the driveway, black wrought iron railings supporting the front porch, Mother's beautiful roses wafting in the breeze, and concluded that life was very good for the Al Bells.

The old apple tree outside my bedroom window supplied more than enough apples for Mother to make canned apples and apple butter, plus pies and my favorite, apple crisp; the peach trees bore delectable peaches, plus, we had a big strawberry patch. We felt decadent, eating (frozen) fresh peaches and strawberries in the middle of winter. Behind the basement stairs, shelves of home-canned beans and tomatoes waited for winter meals, and the freezer was stacked with pork and beef roasts, bacon, sausage, hamburger, chickens, and two kinds of ice cream for Daddy. It seemed that we lived in the Garden of Eden.

What we had was the result of sacrifice and months of manual labor. We never forgot the early days of living in a garage, using an outhouse, and living in a basement with a concrete floor, but we felt blessed all the same. We kids worked hard outside all summer, mowing, weeding the garden, picking strawberries, pulling cockleburrs, horseweeds, and milkweeds out of bean and cornfields. We followed the tractor after the corn was harvested, and picked up bushels of loose ears of corn that had missed the wagon. We carried bales of hay, five gallon buckets of feed – all the things that farm kids did in those days. We worked hard, and we played hard.

One Christmas, when we were still living in the basement, Daddy came up with a very creative decoration for the house. I had been given a Christmas coloring book which included a wonderful drawing of Santa Claus with an overflowing bag of toys, just as he was descending down a chimney. Daddy was very artistic, but he looked at that picture, asked me politely if he could have it, and then proceeded to enlarge it by means of drawing graph lines over it.

The project required a lot of paper, but eventually, he had finished a life-size drawing of Santa Claus. He then placed it over a sheet of plywood, traced it, and began the arduous job of cutting it out with a jig saw. Al Bell's Santa Claus was painted a vivid red and white; the bag was brown with blue and yellow toys popping out of the top. And then began the hardest part: putting it on the roof.

With Allen's help (and much gasping from Mother), Santa was finally set in place right next to our chimney. A floodlight installed at the base of the scene was the finishing touch. It was a quarter of a mile from the corner to our house, and Santa was clearly visible from that distance. We heard stories that folks drove by to see it.

Mother's Friday night tradition of blinking the porch light when she saw Al Bell driving down the hill from the corner changed at Christmas. It was Santa's light that blinked on that last Friday night before Christmas. When Daddy returned home from his last programs, he could, indeed, feel he was on Christmas vacation. It meant a lot to Daddy to see that spectacle (from the corner where the old one room schoolhouse had been); he was reassured that his family waited anxiously to spend a week or two with him, making up for lost time.

Christmas morning on the farm - Allen, Daddy and Rhea.

# Chapter Four

The Bells have been and still are, despite allergies, animal lovers. In addition to our ferocious basset hounds on the farm, we had a variety of barn cats (a few named Tom), a small herd of cattle (in the early years they had names), four to eight hogs, and fifty or so chickens. We sold eggs at the local "Creamery"; I was the lucky recipient who got to wash dozens of eggs every Saturday morning. I know some of you shared this duty, too. It was pretty disgusting. Later on, Daddy added honey bees, Bantam chickens, and a few geese, but we never had a horse.

Cowboy programs and movies were all the rage, and although "The Lone Ranger" was my favorite, I'd watch anything with horses. My fantasy setup during the movie really helped create the mood, too. Pulling a dining room chair into the living room and setting it backwards, as close to the TV as I could get, I added a pillow for a saddle, two tin cans of soup from the kitchen for my stirrups, and one of Daddy's leather belts from his closet for the reins. Straddling the chair, I would twist the belt back and forth during the movie, so I could create that "oater" sound of shifting back and forth in the saddle

Like many children, we Bell kids had been begging to get a horse ever since we moved to the farm. Rhea and Allen told me to forget it, since they had spent their childhood asking for that phantom creature. But the July I was eight years old, my father took me through the horse barn at the Adair County Fair. "Which one do you like the most?" he asked. We played this game a lot, of course; my mom called the Monkey Wards catalog the "Wish Book". This time, however, Daddy had decided that after the oats money came in, we could afford to buy a horse.

Being inside the fair horse barn was heaven to me — the animals' snorting, their soft noses on my rough little hand, the hay smell — yes, even the manure aroma was pleasant to my nose. "Which one do you like the most, Becky Sue?" Daddy repeated. I looked from one to the other. Shiny black stallions, Chestnut brown mares, dappled gray and white ponies. I finally pointed at a smaller horse near me. "Good choice," he said. "That's a Welsh pony, a good size for you and Doug."

I floated through June. Every few days, I'd ask, "Is it time to harvest the oats yet?" Mother cleverly motivated her sleepy little girl to get up one morning by announcing that today was the day. "The oats are going to be harvested today, Becky Sue".

"Any time now," I chanted. "Any time now Daddy's going to bring me home my pony."

Three days later, my dad scolded me harshly for being responsible for the burned out yard light. "If only you would do your chores as soon as you get home from school while it's still light out! But no, you and Doug watch TV until the sun goes down, and then you have to use the big yard light. And now it's burned out, and it's your fault!" I felt guilty, but didn't appreciate why it was such a big deal. However, when I saw my brother holding the tallest ladder we owned against the light pole, I began to worry. Allen was holding the replacement bulb while my dad removed the old bulb. The rest of us were in the house, when suddenly, Allen yelled something at the top of his lungs. We rushed out to the barnyard to find Daddy lying crumpled on the ground. He had fallen off the ladder, twenty-five feet below. Allen was sobbing beside him, thinking he had somehow killed him.

In visible shock, Mother ran back into the house to call the doctor. Now, these were the days of party line phones. Mother had finally gotten used to this intrusion in her life, but being a city girl, she didn't like her privacy being invaded. When she picked up the receiver, two older ladies were slowly discussing their gardens. Mother interrupted, "Please get off the line! This is an emergency! Al Bell just fell off the light pole!" Later, these dear women called all our neighbors on the party line, and told them to get to our house immediately. (From that point on, Mother was patient and gracious, regarding that old phone.)

When Dr. Dolyak, our family doctor, an osteopath, heard my mother's shaking voice tell what had transpired, he refused to send for an ambulance. He was sure that my dad would never make it to the hospital. Minutes later, the doctor arrived from his practice in nearby Stuart, and was surprised that Al Bell was still alive. He directed our neighbors who had gathered around Daddy, to form a woven stretcher with their fingers carefully intertwined under Daddy's body. Mother heard bones cracking as they slowly picked him up, and she led the procession into the house. Rhea, Allen and I had seen my father's ashen face, and we trembled visibly as we followed the group into our folks' bedroom. Mother was concerned about Daddy's breathing, which was so shallow even the doctor had a hard time making it out. I heard one of the neighbors whisper something about Daddy's bad heart. Then one of the wives told me to go to my room and wait, where I threw myself into my closet. "Dear God," I cried, "please don't let Daddy die! It's all my fault that he had to go up on the pole!" I vaguely remember Rhea coming in, crying, and I wondered if she had heard me confess to the crime. I finally got out my apology, and she assured me that it was definitely NOT my fault. It was nobody's fault, but I didn't believe her, and stayed in my room for a long time. In later years, Rhea told me that she, Mother, and Allen also felt guilty that day, all for their own particular reasons.

The men had set Daddy down flat on the bed, per the doctor's orders, and most had gone back outside, but our closest neighbor, Herb Cunningham, stayed nearby, in case he could do anything for his friend, Al Bell. Dr. Dolyak told my mom that most of Daddy's ribs were crushed, and he could only guess at the condition of Daddy's internal organs. The doctor ordered my dad not to move at all. His back was broken for sure, and if Al Bell lived, he could expect to be paralyzed. For the next six weeks, we waited hand and foot on our dad as he withstood terrible pain and the frustrations of not being able to move. He lay flat on his bed, morning to night, while his bones either mended or didn't. It wasn't long before he was joking with us, though, so we knew he was feeling better. Daddy also told us that this was a big reason to believe in God; he'd been praying since he hit the ground that he could do his shows by September, and, thank God, now he knew he would.

Our generous neighbors took over all the farm work which floored my mother, and brought my dad to tears several times. By mid-August, Daddy was walking a little and nagging at Mother to set up his editing and splicing machine on the dining room table. They had traveled to Ireland in June, and he was ready to finish the film. His back hurt horribly, twirling the film back and forth between the reels, then bending over a small very bright bulb with a small magnifier to see the frames up close. He kept at it, cutting and splicing, until he was ready to bring out the projector to add sound and music. This was the process where my folks bickered constantly, but we kids could tell that Mother was lowering her standards a tad, when she'd mutter and shake her head on her way back to the kitchen. Daddy had a long fuse when it came to his temper, but his aching body and time constraints shortened that fuse considerably. He was determined not to cancel the first shows coming up in just days.

Al Bell may have started his assembly programs a couple days late that year, and his body tired easily, but those hundreds of kids sat mesmerized at this dynamic entertainer in his beige cable sweater and brown tam, gesturing with a shillelagh, and mimicking an angry Irishman, as he paced the length of the gymnasium stage.

Of course, all the expenses of the doctor visits and mounds of pain pills were covered by the oats money. I never got a horse. In fact, I never mentioned wanting one after that. But I learned that unceasing prayers can and do work. Al Bell carried on grandly in Iowa's schools for another twenty-five years.

# Chapter Five

One of the funniest things Al Bell ever did on the farm had to do with leftover pink paint. Mother decided that she wanted the black wrought iron railings on the porch to be painted pink. (It was the 1950's, and the color pink was really popular.) After the job was done, Daddy announced that he had definitely mixed too much pink paint, so he looked around to see what else could benefit from that lovely color. He started with the pump in the front yard, and ended with his antique manure spreader that sat out in the barnyard. The neighbors hooted and hollered, of course; we all considered it to be hilarious. It was the prettiest manure spreader in four counties.

When my brother Allen was a senior at Menlo High School, my mother volunteered to chaperone his class on their senior trip to Chicago. They were gone for three days, and I was in charge of keeping it together at home. Mother had made up some meals for me to defrost and encouraged me to make a dessert if I wanted. I was in the sixth grade, quite plump, so I decided to make a diet cake from one of my mom's new cookbooks. It was chocolate, but with no eggs, and the secret ingredient was coffee. I mixed it up, baked it, and it didn't come out very high. In fact, it was about one inch high. The coffee grounds sunk to the bottom, but I knew Daddy liked coffee, so I thought that would be okay.

After dinner, I told him I had made a cake for him, and he was proud of me. "Give me a big piece!" I watched as my dad took the big first bite; coffee grounds fell back onto the plate, but he had ingested enough to be practically choking, and managed to spit out, "Water! I need a drink!" Bless his heart, he ate the whole cake, and told me it was wonderful. When Mother returned home to hear the story, she laughed and laughed. "You're supposed to make a cup of coffee, Sweetie, so it's liquid when you add it to the cake. But that was a good girl to make dessert for your daddy." I learned from my mistake, and went on to (eventually) become a good cook.

The day before Mother and Allen returned from their trip, Daddy suffered a terrible accident. Every night back then, Daddy would bring in the milk from the barn and employ our aluminum separator downstairs. The separator was a strange looking machine, with a big spout on top to funnel out the milk, and a smaller spout below to handle just the heavier cream which had been separated from the milk. (Daddy loved cream, but most of it – can you imagine? – was taken out and poured into the hog trough!) When the separator was running at its high speed, fluid flowed out the spouts into containers. I would wash the separator parts afterwards, and then it would be reassembled for the next night.

It was our last night of "batching" it before Mother and Allen came home; I was upstairs, washing our supper dishes. Daddy was in the basement, running the separator. Suddenly, I heard a horrible grinding noise, and then a series of crashes, as the separator came apart, and metal parts were hurled around the room. Daddy had made a sound I couldn't define, but I knew it wasn't good. I ran down the stairs, and there lay my dad on the concrete floor, bleeding profusely from his mouth. The machine had driven metal parts into my dad's face, teeth were missing, and he seemed to be in shock. "Daddy! Daddy!" I cried, helplessly.

With some difficulty, my father stood up and said weakly, "Get some towels. Get Doug. We have to go to the hospital." It was hard for him to talk, and just as hard to understand what he said, but I got the gist of it and ran upstairs. Using the old crank telephone in the basement, he called the hospital in Dexter and let them know we were coming. His hands, arms, and chest had been cut, too, but he held himself together with the towels, and we were off to Dexter. I have no idea how he was able to drive, but I remember talking to him all the way there. He looked like he'd just walked out of a horror movie. Many stitches and bandages later, we were back home, and my dad went straight to bed. I assume he was given pain medication. I lay in my bed, worrying about what Mother would think. Was it possible that I was to blame in some way?

The next morning, Daddy assured me that he was to blame

for the accident. He hadn't assembled the separator correctly. The machine was destroyed, of course, and as we cleaned up the basement, my father told me how he'd been thinking of giving up the milk cows anyway. From then on, we raised only beef cattle. Daddy's dental work required many visits, and he bore the scars from that accident for the rest of his life.

Doug on the farm, 1961. This was before Daddy added the breezeway and garage.

Daddy and mother before leaving for Hawaii, 1958. They left Doug and me with my aunt's family in Orange, CA.

## Chapter Six

Daddy had a penchant for naming all the animals on the farm. He began with our first cow, a pretty Holstein, who supplied us with milk and cream in the early years. Perhaps Mother named her; after all; the cow's moniker was "Chloe" which was my Mother's favorite old song. We had another milk cow, a soft beige Guernsey with white trim who, I believe, was named Daisy. I was pretty young at this time, but I distinctly remember her first calf trying to mount me, as I played with her second calf on the barn floor. This hideous business was indeed alarming to me, and I had to scream for Daddy to get the gangly, heavy thing off me. Cows had such gorgeous eyes that I couldn't resist gazing into them, as they fluttered their long, thick lashes back at me. When Daddy decided to go strictly with Angus, the premier beef cattle, he began with "Belle" who had "Beau". Al Bell was always a player of words and rhymes, so this alliteration continued until the herd was too numerous to name.

I don't remember any of the hogs' names, but I'm sure that the first few were named, as well. Baby chickens were adorable, but they all looked alike after they grew their white feathers, so they remained nameless.

Now, the barn cats were different. Since our childhood conversations often included tales of kitties, many were named. I recall that most yellow toms were called "Tom", unless we had more than one, in which case, the second might be "Tommy" or "Tom Two". As much as the felines begged for attention, only one ever became a house pet.

One hot summer afternoon, Daddy had been mowing the long grass in our ditches outside the gate. Too late, he spied one of our cats lying in the ditch. This yellow "Tom" lost two legs from the mower.

My dad gathered him up, gory bloody stumps streaming cat blood down Daddy's arms and hands. The poor thing was in shock. My dad gently brought him into the kitchen for cleanup and examination. Mother didn't think the cat would live, but Daddy's constant care and medical attention kept "Crippie" Chauncey, The Second, who traveled to Alaska with us. alive for a couple years. Obviously, his name came from the distinct hobble the pathetic animal learned, as a result of losing one whole leg and a part of the one on the opposite side in the back. He became Daddy's little buddy. Somewhere I have a picture of Crippie curled up in Daddy's lap as we watched "Gunsmoke".

The single barnyard cat whose memory can still bring tears to my eyes was "Grandma" kitty. "Grandma" was just a young, gray-striped cat when we first moved to the farm. She bore many generations of gray-striped and yellow cats, but she outlived them all. "Grandma" was an extraordinary mouser, for which she won Daddy's heart and admiration. He would pick her up frequently, pet her, and tell her what a good cat she was, and in return, she followed Daddy as he worked around the barnyard. Many, many years later, around eighteen years later, Mother and Daddy had sold the farm, moved to town, but came back one afternoon to say hello to the new owners, and to see the old place.

As Daddy stood in the driveway, entertaining the young farm couple, he happened to hear a meow coming from the barn. Looking up, he saw "Grandma" kitty running toward him, and crying loudly. The tears leapt from my father's eyes, as he petted the scrawny bag of bones that was "Grandma" cat. She wound lovingly around and between his ankles as he baby talked to her. Al Bell was so moved that he had a hard time leaving the farm. Reluctantly, he pulled out of the driveway, and looking in his rear view mirror, saw "Grandma" settle back on her haunches and watch him exit from her life again. Her devotion touched my mother as well, as this was one of Mother's favorite farm anecdotes for many years after my dad's death.

## Chapter Seven

Barn owls were common on the farm; their evening hoots lent a lonesome, rural flavor to sweet June nights, as well as snowy ones in March. Bright red cardinals posed on snow-covered bushes, waiting for a photographer to put them on a magazine cover. Red-headed woodpeckers accented quiet days with their rat-a-tats on telephone poles. Every pasture sang with the warbled, "See me, I'm a meadowlark". And purple martins devoured mosquitos.

That's why my father spent two days assembling a martin house that would stand for many years near the big propane gas tank by the garage. He knew that martins live in a communal situation, so this was a rather large birdhouse. And with Daddy's creative twist on things, he did what he had done when we lived in Ames. The birdhouse was a replica of our house, a T-design. After suffering multitudinous mosquito bites down at the pond on many of our dusk picnics, we all clamored for our dad to build Martin House II. And he did. A two story birdhouse set upon a tall post, watched over the water for many years; after all, there were many more bloodsuckers down at the pond. Martins came from all over Adair County to move in.

The bloodsuckers, Genus II, were leeches. If you've ever watched the wonderful film, "African Queen" with Humphrey Bogart and Katherine Hepburn, you've seen what leeches look like. Big, nasty, black worms that prefer to attach themselves to your body – UNDER your bathing suit. And you have to be careful how you take them off. Yucck! I shudder as I write. Why would you go swimming in a pond that has leeches? Have you worked all day in the blistering sun, baling hay? The refreshing relief from a farm pond is too tempting. The miserable creatures were not always in the pond when we were swimming.  In fact, I don't remember them at all when we swam down there in later years.  (To the north of where I currently live, back in the deep green fir forests, there is a lake named Leech Lake.  I'll bet it's just for fishing.)

When we were helping Daddy build the dock on the pond (which had been a three acre lake until a couple acres of Harvey Payton's soil washed down the hill to eventually fill it up), we all were taught a hard lesson.  First, if you've never worked with creosote, try not to.  Daddy had to coat the long posts for the dock with black, sticky, smelly creosote, and then stressed that we really shouldn't touch the creosote, if at all possible.  We soon found out why.  While our dad pounded on the top of the post to sink the pole into the mud, we kids had to try to keep the bobbing post in one place.  In our swimming suits, treading water and finally, submerging for the longest posts, we had to grab that sticky, stinky pole with our entire bodies and push down.

As soon as we had finally set the poles, and we emerged from the water, our bodies began to burn.  Our flesh was dark red with heat, and there was no relief, except to stay in the water.  By nightfall, the dock was done, and we kids cried out on our long walk back up to the house that our skin was burning us alive.  Mother gathered us in the bathroom and scrubbed off the creosote with hot (!) soapy water, promising us that we really would feel better once it was off our skin.  What an ordeal!  My dad waited outside until it was his turn for a bath, and not one word of complaint came out of his mouth.  "Don't you hurt, Daddy?" I finally asked as we passed each other in the hallway.

"Oh, it's not bad, but I'm sure sorry you kids got it all over you." Of course, his skin was burning up too, as he had to hold the pole in place from the top by grasping it with one arm, and his bare chest and stomach.  His skin was as red as ours, but the only whining came from the peanut gallery.

As I have mentioned elsewhere, my dad was an avid fisherman.  When we traveled, he fished for trout from clear, rushing streams, using various sizes and colors of flies from his collection.  He caught catfish when he and his young family lived on the Mississippi River (several years before I was born).  One of the reasons he wanted this pond was so that he could fish.  The government had helped finance our pond for ecological reasons.  A leg of the Middle River flowed through our property, just a rivulet at times, but after rains, it became a muddy current rushing over tall grass on either side.  By building a dam on a descending slope of one field, this valuable resource was "controlled". We actually had a beaver dam at one time. Birds, from mallards to blue herons, stopped at this wildlife sanctuary and stayed until late fall. My dad and brothers hunted from a duck blind nestled into one corner of the pond and provided a Canadian goose for Thanksgiving dinner. In winter, we ice skated. The rest of the year, we fished and swam.

The pond was stocked with fish. Daddy requested catfish, sunfish, and bluegills; the latter two were "pretty." With time, as the pond filled in, the bullheads took over. Mother fried them all up, and many a pleasant picnic down at the pond had a variety of small, but tasty fillets. Fish was not my mother's favorite meat, but after she suffered a choking accident, she never ate it again. When she finally stopped choking, she told us hoarsely, that the bone was lodged in her throat, and that bone stayed in her throat for three long days! (She had gone to the doctor who assured her that the bone would eventually dissolve and go down. Thanks, Doc!)

Daddy had taught Doug and me to fish with long cane poles. I remember this as "Jerk" fishing. Hanging the pole over the dock, and tossing the line out with its cute little red and white bobber, and a big fat night crawler on the hook, weighted with a small sinker, we would wait for a "hit". We learned the technique unique to pole fishing – to wait for the bobber to go down a third time, and then "JERK!" the pole out of the water, bringing up, hopefully, a fish on the other end.

If you've never taken a bullhead off a fishing hook, don't do it. It's very tricky. I went through many bloody fingers before I got the hang of it. "Bring the hook out the same way it went in" Daddy's voice instructed, time and again.

I was very fortunate that my dad liked my company. I was terribly shy as a girl, and not confident that I had anything valuable to offer, conversation-wise. (My sister was, and still is, very talkative. She's like my dad in many ways – gregarious and chatty.) But when my dad was on leave from his grueling school schedule and that constant pressure of being "on" all the time, he came home to be replenished. He wanted peace and quiet. Thus, he spent many hours alone on his tractor, or in walking the fence line, looking for holes to repair. And for a couple years, when I was eleven or so, he asked me to go fishing with him. I was very flattered. Despite my lazy morning habits, I would jump out of bed before five o'clock. It was still dark, but I would find my dad, waiting in the kitchen. Daddy and I would then grab our poles, a can of worms, and meander down to the pond. Sitting on the dock on those misty summer mornings, feeling the first glow of the sun on our backs, was paradise. We didn't talk much. We just sat together and fished. It was "our" time, and I didn't get enough of that, in my spoiled opinion.

All of us kids played basketball, so Al Bell put a hoop up on the wall of the second floor of the old barn, one of the original buildings from the previous owner. When the barn was stacked with sweet-smelling hay, it was easy to jump from bale to bale to get up to that floor. It became more adventurous as the bales disappeared throughout the winter, (having been tossed down for the cows in their manger), but all four of us spent hours perfecting our free throws, hook shots, playing "Horse", "Around the World" and "Twenty One". The rickety floor with missing slats provided even more of a challenge. Once in a while, dribbling in for a lay up, an old board would finally crack, and a foot would plunge through the floor. Mother made sure we were up on our tetanus shots.

Our basketball area was actually quite small; it wasn't big enough to scrimmage, or to take more than two lay up steps. But shooting hoops became cheap therapy after a long day at school, or a reward after working all day on the farm. Freezing weather didn't deter us, either. It was amazing how fast we warmed up while shooting baskets. First, we'd lose our hats and gloves; within minutes, our bulky coats were thrown on a nearby bale. Flannel shirts and sweatshirts were perfect until we climbed down from the hayloft, perspiring, and realized that it was still just twenty degrees outside.

Doug and I on our frozen pond, 1959.

## Chapter Eight

"Sons of Gaspe (Gas-pay)", the third Al Bell film, was done primarily in the Canadian provinces of Quebec and Nova Scotia in June of 1951. The entire family traveled from our home in Ames; my little brother was a baby, I was five years old, Allen was eleven and Rhea would turn thirteen while we were filming. I wasn't old enough to appreciate the artistic framework Daddy wove throughout the movie, but upon viewing it as an adult, I was astounded. This was nothing like Al Bell's later movies; his narration included him reciting "Evangeline", a classic poem by Longfellow set in Quebec. My dad's reading was dramatic and sensitive, lending a dark, romantic aura to the rocky coast and hilly countryside.

Highlights from the movie included the Bay of Fundy, one of two tidal bores in North America, deep sea fishing, the French-speaking, rather European communities with white-aproned women sliding bread dough on long trays into large, outdoor ovens, and oversized St. Bernard dogs pulling carts. Highlights from our trip included a pancake-eating contest at a restaurant en route to Quebec (Daddy and Allen finished in a dead heat), little Doug's sickly condition which encouraged the other three of us to finish off his baby food. ("We shouldn't waste it!" – my mom), and one more daily challenge: Rhea, Allen and I were to stay in the car and gladly consume a constant breakfast diet of oranges and powdered sugar donuts. While my parents ate bacon and eggs inside a nearby café, we kids were sticky from "gold nuggets" (Allen's term) and covered in powdered sugar. None of us could face that breakfast combination ever again. I also remember a terrible rainstorm soaking us in our tent one night, and being filmed, running endlessly around a huge boulder in a scene made expressly for comic relief.

Al Bell decided what the program needed that year was a genuine St. Bernard. "Jacques" was purchased before we left Quebec and stuffed in the back seat with Rhea, Allen and myself. It became obvious right away that this monster would sit where he pleased, and he chose a window seat. The closer to Iowa we got, the hotter it was in the car. Previously, Rhea and Allen had each taken the window seats. I was left to balance in the middle where I could lean over the front seat and complain to my parents about my mistreatment from my brother Allen, a huge tease (as most older brothers are). However, the addition of Jacques to the mix changed the lineup. Because St. Bernards are famous for drooling, especially when they become hot, I found myself relocated next to Jacques, as a buffer for my siblings. Both Rhea and Allen were disgusted by the long strings of saliva that blew inside the car, as Jacques stuck his hot head out the window. I would have been disgusted myself, except for the fact that I was covered with drool, and merely felt nauseous. I had no choice but to lean out the window myself, so that I could breathe, and as a result, Jacques and I grew to be very close. At five years old, my vote didn't count for much; the trip home seemed interminable.

Once we were home, I didn't hang out with Jacques much, but as Doug grew into a toddler, Jacques allowed him to ride on his back. "Ride 'em, cowboy!" When Daddy returned to the schools in September, Jacques traveled with him, of course, but now he sported a big bib under his chin. Someone – a principal perhaps – offered to buy Jacques, and he was gone by the end of the school year.

"Hootchie", Daddy's name for the pizote that he purchased for the Central America movie, was the most mischievous pet we ever owned. A hyper-active raccoon-like animal, Hootchie got into absolutely everything in the house: into Doug's baby food, into Daddy's pocket for cigarettes, into kitchen drawers, under beds, on top of high shelves. "Where's Hootchie?" became a battle cry. Left to his own devices, he was capable of destroying clothes, furniture, cars. He was, undeniably, cute. His antics were hilarious. With a curious little nose and bright, black eyes, he would look at you innocently, while planning his next devastation. Daddy taught him to sit on his shoulder and do tricks, especially with the cigarettes in Daddy's suit pocket. You had to watch him closely, though, or he would eat them.

Hootchie was a big hit at the schools. Daddy kept him on a leash, so his monkey-like gymnastics were basically under control.

He performed most of his tricks perched on Daddy's shoulder, as kids watched, spellbound. While the Central America film was being run, Hootchie was safely ensconced in his cage. None of us were too sad at the end of the school year when someone bought Hootchie. Daddy missed him, but the scars from his claws on all of us were a reminder that a pizote is basically a wild animal.

The attention getter in "Sons of Okefenokee" (a national swamp park in Georgia) was the threat of alligators. Daddy emphasized in his lecture how this frighteningly primitive reptile did not just reside quietly in dark, murky waters. Two or three scenes in the film demonstrate their ability to stand on all fours when duly motivated, and rush, running, onto dry land. This makes the alligator really, really scary. My dad decided that he had to show an alligator to the school kids back in Iowa.

So, we were given a baby alligator by park management, and our trip home became quite interesting. "Ally" resided in a large waterproof container, complete with rocks and water, at our feet on the floor of the back seat. A makeshift lid set on top of his box most of the time, but his presence was just too titillating for Doug and me. We'd bring him out of the box and hold him really close to our faces so we could appreciate his long snout and big teeth. We discovered how sharp his teeth were every time we brought him out of the box, however. The little bugger didn't care for being played with, and his natural instinct was to snap at the nearest soft flesh, usually our fingers. "Put him back," our folks must have said a dozen times a day. "Where'd he go?" was another hair-raising question.

Ally Gator was a huge attraction for Daddy's programs. Daddy learned to hold him by the end of his tail, so kids could see him up close without the danger of Al Bell's fingers being chewed on, but as the reptile inevitably grew larger, the danger grew anyway. Solution? Get another newborn. Where? Believe it or not, from the Wards or Sears catalog! They weren't that expensive, and they arrived as tiny babies. After losing the second one almost immediately upon arrival, Daddy learned that he'd better order two at a time, so there would always be a backup. Yes, we went through many of them, mostly because of the frigid weather. On weekends, baby alligators resided in our old fish aquarium, set on the kitchen table with a warm floodlight attached. Those dark green snappers would bask in the light all day, as if they were sunbathing, but during Iowa's frozen nights, a couple of the smaller babies didn't make it through the night.

Now, we all know and accept that, in today's enlightened world, wild animals, like alligators, have no place in the home. The lack of regulations in the 1950's made it too easy, however, for anyone to own all sorts of exotic critters. Remember the urban legend about giant alligators in the sewers of New York City? I'm not so sure it wasn't true…

Dogs were a much more practical companion for Daddy to have on the road. One of my personal favorites from Al Bell's films is "Sons of Chinook", starring my brother, Allen. This adventure, set around Calgary, Canada and the gorgeous Banff, Jasper, and Glacier National Parks, featured Daddy as an evil villain, complete with black hat and full, dark beard. I thought he was handsome, but then I've always been partial to beards. (I didn't know until Al Bell came to my own school, that Daddy had encouraged audiences to boo and hiss at the villain.) My brother Allen's stalwart companion in the film was our real-life dog, Maggie, a smart, sweet basset hound. Maggie was given to Daddy's cousin, a basset hound breeder because of her "great lines" and good temperament, with the condition that one of her descendents would always be our faithful watch dog. Strangely, we named all of them (I remember three), "Chauncey". Not that "Chauncey" isn't a wonderful British name, but I never could appreciate why my parents didn't opt for different names with each basset puppy. Perhaps it had to do with the tradition in the Bell family of naming all the males, "William" (followed by their middle name which generally was the name they preferred to be called – thus William Allen Bell the second, my brother, went by "Allen".). It was confusing, though, when the family reminisced about "Chauncey". "Which Chauncey?" "Oh, Chauncy the second," came the answer.

In the summer of 1960, after we returned from filming "Sons of Alaska", Daddy tracked down a breeder of Huskies. Al Bell had learned his lesson about bringing animals home from the trip. Our new dog, "Shleekai", had an Eskimo name, plus one blue eye and one brown eye. In the days when most folks owned beagles and spaniels, this was one spooky-looking husky. The fact that he was terribly skittish didn't help, either. Nevertheless, Daddy taught him sled dog commands and a few commands in Eskimo, and the two were ready to embark on another school year.

I'm sure that Daddy bonded with Shleekai on the road, although

I know the husky wasn't a favorite. We all surmised that Shleekai was not as smart as other dogs we had known and loved. He was such a reluctant, slow learner – and too rowdy to settle down. Fortunately, at the end of his run appearing with Al Bell, he, too, was sold to someone who had "always wanted a husky".

"Sons of Newfoundland" (pronounced NEW-fund-LAND') brought us face to face with the wonderful Newfoundland dog. These days, huskies and Newfoundland dogs are fairly common, but both breeds were rare in Iowa back then. "Me Too" was sweet, affectionate, coal black with gobs of curly hair, and extremely large. The unique feature of the Newfoundland dog is its webbed feet which allow it to be an extraordinary swimmer. Living on an island like Newfoundland, which is located off eastern Canada's coast, being able to swim well would definitely be an asset.

We kids didn't really get to spend much time with Daddy's "show" dogs. Our father was on the road most of the time, and once he had trained them, he preferred that we stick to playing with "Chauncey". (I know, "Which Chauncey?")

One of the most beautiful animals Daddy ever took on the road was "Pedro", the colorful macaw. A member of the parrot family, macaws are quite large, with a very long tail, a brilliant crest, and a terribly sharp beak. Daddy bore the scars from Pedro for a long time, but Pedro learned all kinds of English phrases, so he was the perfect show-off for Daddy's lecture. A talking bird draws almost anyone to it, and gobs of kids would crowd around Daddy after the program, "Make him talk! Make him talk!" Pedro was purchased for the "Sons of Galapagos" movie, but macaws are found in the jungles of Central America and Mexico, as well as South America. With the passing of time, even macaws have become a popular pet. Old Pedro became more and more difficult to handle. He was finally donated to the Des Moines Zoo, where they made a special sign and cage for Pedro. It was sad to visit him. He lived for a long time, of course, but to see this gorgeous bird in a zoo cage was hard. He still talked, to no one in particular. When my folks visited him on occasion, it was obvious that Pedro remembered them. It was difficult for Daddy to leave him. Of course, it was the best thing for Pedro to be with animal trainers who knew better than we how to handle him.

The most remembered pet from the Al Bell shows is apparently "Ping Lee Ho", a purebred Chow-Chow. Many of the comments on the Al Bell Facebook page recall "the dog with the purple tongue". Indeed, chows are born with purple tongues, and even my own Buddy Sue, a chow mix, had a purple tongue. I see chow-chows frequently now; black are common. Ping Lee was the red variety: large body, very furry, a bushy tail that curls over the back, pointy ears with a "pinched-looking" face, and eyes that are actually almond shaped. Ping Lee became more Mother's dog, as she was traveling with Daddy by the time they visited Hong Kong. Even though all dogs love me, Ping Lee would growl whenever I visited my parents. Mother admitted that he really was a one-woman dog. She was quite attached to Ping Lee, and she missed him for a long time.

Because the Al Bell program animals were seen by so many people over the years, most of them were adopted. Looking back, it's a shame that Daddy's show animals were adopted for a specific purpose, and then let go after their purpose was fulfilled. Let us conclude with, "We all knew much better later", and continue to fight for animal rights.

Al Bell and "Hootchie".

## Chapter Nine

*(Chapters 9-14 were transcribed from tapes made by Al Bell, circa 1974-1975)*

"WHO'S SITTING IN MY LAP?" the little boy screamed, as he ran down the stairs into the living room. He rushed up to his beloved mother and glared at the tiny baby nestled in her lap. His brother, Lloyd had just arrived in the world. "That's the first thing I remember," said my father, as he talked about his childhood. "That baby turned out to be my companion for years and years in life."

William Lloyd Bell, the boys' father, was employed as first cashier at the bank in Lost Nation, a small town of about five hundred people in eastern Iowa. (The bank later went broke in 1921, along with most of the banks in the country in the "Flash Depression".) The folks in Lost Nation said that "Bill" Bell always had a good word to say for everybody. When the meanest man in town died, a fellow walked up to Bill and asked deviously, "Say, Bill. What did you think of Old John who just passed away?" Grandpa Bell paused and reflected for a few seconds, and then slowly drawled, "Well, he was an awfully good whistler."

Daddy's mother's name was Maude Evelyn Robbins which is a good old-fashioned moniker. She had been a school teacher in La Rose, Illinois, before she married Lloyd. They met somewhere around Washburn, Iowa, where Grandpa's father owned a hardware store. "The Bell house is still standing in Lost Nation; it's on the southwest side of town." Daddy continued, "Originally, it was white stucco, but it's painted now."

As Al Bell always said, he was born "at a very early age." As a matter of fact, it was a little earlier than usual. His father owned a Stanley Steamer which was an early automobile powered by an external combustion engine. Grandma Bell was expecting Daddy, and one day, Grandpa took her riding in the Stanley Steamer. It was a hot July day, and they laughed and talked as they roamed the countryside. Unfortunately, Grandpa forgot about the very bumpy railroad crossing ahead. He hit the crossing with those semi-pneumatic tires so hard, that when they got across, Grandma said very quietly, "Lloyd, I think you'd better take me to the hospital." Al Bell was born very soon thereafter.

Upstairs in the Bell house was a guest room, and it was very cold in the wintertime. Daddy remembers that his mother kept Christmas candy on the dresser in that room. It was "wonderful, pink divinity." Daddy confessed to creeping stealthily into the cold room and stealing a piece or two before Christmas. In the hall upstairs, there was a clothes chute that descended to the basement. One Christmas, little Allen became very curious about Santa Claus and asked his mother, "How does Santa get into our house?" His mother answered, "He goes through the clothes chute down into the rest of the house and out through the chimney." Sure enough, the night before Christmas that year, her son caught a glimpse of Santa, disappearing down the clothes chute.

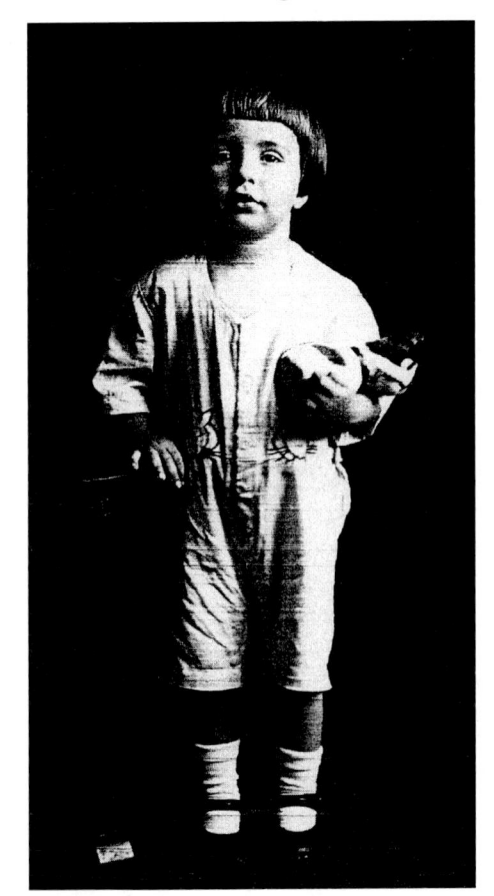

Great Grandma Bell, Lloyd's mother, came to visit for a while. She was almost seventy but she brought a gift for her grandson, Allen. It was a motorcycle with a motorcyclist perched on the seat. The miniature driver had on a beautiful red outfit for riding. The motorcycle had a spring motor, and it zoomed around the living room floor while Al Bell watched in fascination. When it started to fall, the stand on the side would

A very young Al Bell, circa 1918.

catch it from tipping over. (Daddy still had it when we were kids. It would probably work today.)

In 1918, the Bells traveled to Maquoketa to celebrate the end of World War One. A huge parade was held with all the returning soldiers. It was so colorful and vivid that Daddy, who was only three years old, could remember one particular float. A dummy stuffed with straw, in a full German uniform complete with helmet, was surrounded by three real American soldiers. The soldiers, who had bayonets on the ends of their rifles, were hitting and stabbing "the Kaiser." It had quite a dramatic effect on everyone, especially little Allen Bell.

Right across the street from the Bells lived a family by the name of Kagebine. Allen and his little brother went over there frequently because Mr. Kagebine owned a Franklin automobile. He would explain to the two boys that his car was "air-cooled". It had no radiator. The Bell brothers would nod their heads up and down very wisely, but of course, they didn't understand a word of it.

Speaking of cars, Grandpa Bell drove a Winston-6 for a while which had semi-pneumatic tires. One afternoon he roared into the driveway and accidentally ran over his son's foot! Of course, Daddy put on a great act about how his foot had been crushed. Then, after his drama had concluded, he impishly grinned at his father and confessed that he was all right.

Every Sunday, the family dressed up in their finest clothes. They were called "golf" clothes because the family drove out to the Lost Nation golf course. Occasionally his parents would let Allen play, but he was probably a great burden to their game. Daddy remembered that in those days, you had to scoop up a handful of sand from a nearby sandbox, form a cone with it on the ground, and there was your tee!

"I started kindergarten above the bank," my dad reminisced. "There was no room at the school. Mother took me on my first day, and I was home before noon because somebody hurt my feelings!" Daddy freely admitted that his dear mother had doted on him at home, and of course, he loved it.

Al Bell always had a way with the girls. Even as a little boy, the older girls found him charming. In the same neighborhood as the Bells, a well-to-do family by the name of Frazier lived. One of the two sisters, Fern, was going to get married, so she staged a mock wedding. It was a grandiose occasion, and Fern had chosen her friend Allen to be the ring bearer. He was about five years old and quite a performer. Daddy told me that "to this day, she still has the picture of me holding the ring."

One balmy summer afternoon, Al Bell thought of a chivalrous way to woo his current girlfriend. Down the block, a cherry tree was just bursting with ripe, juicy cherries. Daddy bravely climbed up onto a corner post of the fence next to the tree, grabbed onto a nearby branch, and casually began picking the biggest, reddest cherries he could reach. He was very confident as he handed down his bounty to his fair lady standing below. Suddenly, the limb he was holding onto broke and gave way. CRASH! THUMP! Daddy fell to the ground and tore a big gash in his right leg. Completely forgetting his lady love, he screamed out in anguish, and ran, crying, all the way home. Al Bell's Aunt Grace, who was staying with them, was a Christian Scientist, and as Daddy said, "They don't believe much in First Aid." She prayed for his wounded leg, and then just stuck a bandage over it.

Doctor Huff was a very important person in my dad's life. The doctor had an office and his home together on the corner of Main Street. Dr. Huff had predicted that Al Bell wouldn't live to be six years old. His diagnosis was bronchitis, combined with rheumatic fever; however, Grandpa Bell refused to resign his son to that fate. Rather, he fervently set out to cure Allen himself. First, he built a tent with solid floors and beds in the back yard. Then, he and Daddy slept in that tent all spring, summer and fall. Even in winter, when the icy winds whistled outside and snow fell, those two shivered inside the tent. Grandpa's basic idea was to expose his little boy to more oxygen. Amazingly, little Allen's health grew stronger and stronger. By the next spring, his wardrobe became more normal. His dad cut the sleeves off his coats and shirts first, and then his pant legs, by intervals, were chopped off shorter and shorter. By summer, Daddy was wearing shorts and shirts like all the other young boys. Dr Huff may have been stuffed with medical knowledge, but Grandpa was determined to save his son's life. By using common sense and a lot of patience, he did! (Perhaps Grandpa remembered how Teddy Roosevelt similarly slept in a tent to be cured of his health problems. At any rate, this was the holistic method.)

One Christmas when Al Bell was about seven years old, his father came upstairs to his room where Daddy was playing with his new toy train. "Choo-Choo-Choo-Choo. Whoo-Ooh!" It was "the best Santy Claus Christmas" he'd ever had. He didn't even hear his father coming upstairs, but he realized something important was coming when Grandpa solemnly shut the door and sat down on a nearby chair. "Allen," he began. "I think I better tell you…There's no Santa Claus." Allen, being a very sensitive little boy, looked at his train, said nothing, but knew that this was the worst day of his life.

William Lloyd Bell worked at the bank, but every noon he would come home for lunch. One day, little Allen made some sort of mistake in his etiquette at the table. He had used the wrong fork or picked up something with his fingers. His father made him stand in the corner of the kitchen, at which point, Al Bell was heard to mumble "I guess what I need is a book on Emily Post, so I'll know how to behave at dinner!" Obviously, Daddy's early childhood was spent in a "proper" home.

"In the first grade," Daddy explained, "I was very small because of the rheumatic fever and bronchitis." When he was in the second grade, he told me that the bigger kids would stuff snow up his sleeves and down his back on the way home from school. Daddy admitted that, "I'd cry and carry on, and that probably didn't do me any good, either!" Then he smiled wryly, "Are you old enough to remember those ads that showed the skinny kid who gets sand kicked in his face by a big, muscle-bound lifeguard at the beach?"

"Yes!" I replied. "They were on the backs of comic books! Something about being a ninety-seven pound weakling."

"Well I was a fifty-four pound weakling until I got to the fifth grade."

When we kids were growing up, Daddy used to warn us about lying with the following family anecdote: Daddy's younger brother, Lloyd decided to play hooky from school with one of the Drake boys one day. All day he played in a sand pile which was actually very close to their house. Lloyd Senior happened to see Lloyd Junior on his way home at noon, but he waited until after work to corner his younger son. "Well, how was school today?"

"Just fine," little Lloyd answered.

"How'd you like your classes?"

"Oh, just swell."

"How was the teacher today?"

Lloyd was caught up in his story by now, and replied casually, "Dandy!"

"How were the other boys and girls?"

"Oh, fine." Lloyd stretched out his legs like he'd seen his dad do. "What did you study?"

Lloyd, startled, sat up. "Well...Well..."

Finally, his father let the axe fall. "I just want you to know that I saw you today, playing in the sand pile, on my way home at noon. And this will teach you that you have to tell at least three lies to cover up the one you told in the first place!" (My dad's admonishment to us kids used the number seven, not three.)

On Daddy's seventh birthday, his parents gave him a watch that had a steel cover over it, so he wouldn't break the hands or the glass. It was a beautiful watch for a young boy. Close to suppertime, Daddy and his father were sitting at the bottom of the stair landing in the kitchen. Grandpa was cleaning his fingernails with his pearl-handled pocketknife while he tried to teach his son how to tell time. Little Allen could tell twelve and six o'clock easily enough, but any other combination of the short and long hands confused him. His father explained over and over again, until he became so irritated at Allen's inability "to grasp such simple principles" that he lost his temper. Grandpa had a blade open on that pocketknife, and he threw it across the kitchen. The blade stuck into the baseboard on the wall, and the shiny pearl handle just quivered. Evelyn Bell, who was cooking at the stove, was quite shocked, and of course, so was little Allen. Needless to say, the lesson on telling time was over.

Youngsters have always experimented with cigarette smoking, and Daddy was no exception. He and the neighbor boys used to go back behind the barn and smoke tobacco rolled in corn silks. They smoked and smoked and smoked, and eventually became so sick, that they abstained for a long, long time. (Unfortunately, Daddy later became such a heavy smoker that it affected his health, but that comes later in his life story.)

The only Halloween Al Bell remembered from his early childhood was the year a group of pranksters dragged a cow upstairs in the schoolhouse. As if that wasn't enough, they fed the poor creature Epsom salts! "I guess it was a very disastrous occasion," he smiled ruefully and continued. "The same night, that inventive group of adolescents took a buggy apart and then reassembled it on top of the grain elevator! The whole town was quite impressed the next morning."

"One of the most astounding things of my young life was the

summer I conducted my own circus. I was seven." He had conceived the idea when a professional circus came to town. "I began the project by recruiting friends next door at the Reutenbeck home. They were good friends as well as neighbors. Al Bell's eyes shifted to the wall as he remembered. "When I entered the kitchen, Mrs. Reutenbeck was humming and stirring a cake batter at the same time. Since she was so immersed in her cake making, I decided to surprise her and then tell her about my idea for the circus. I sneaked in and hid behind the back door for a few moments, and then when she turned from the table, I jumped out and yelled, 'BOO!' Mrs. Reutenbeck screamed and threw the whole bowl of cake batter up in the air and all over the kitchen!" Luckily for Daddy, his friends responded better to the circus idea.

Al Bell organized a circus at the age of seven, and claimed the title of Ring Master, 1922.

**COMING**
**B.R.B. CIRCUS**
Stupendous Open-Air Attraction
TWO BIG DAYS of THRILLS
Friday and Saturday Afternoons
**JUNE 20-21**
Com. at 2:30
Bell's Back Yard
SEE The Wild, Untamed Mouse-Devouring CATS, Captured in the Rutenbeck Jungles; The Wild Man, a Rare and Ferocious Bi-Ped; Etc., Etc.
VICIOUS GARBAGE HOUNDS
Acrobats in Death-Defying Stunts
**THRILLING**
HAIR-RAISING FEATS IN THE AIR--DON'T MISS IT!
Adults, 5c; Kids, 3c.
Pop Corn, Pink Lemonade, Extra

One of Daddy's friends, Lee Bowman, had a dad who was a printer. Consequently, those posters for Al Bell's circus were mighty impressive. Daddy kept one of the originals that was posted all over Lost Nation, and I think if you had seen it tacked to a wall, you would have come, too. He organized all kinds of races featuring "wild dogs and wild cats", and Al Bell, at seven years old, was the ringmaster. Little Helen Allis from across the street was the gypsy fortuneteller. In fact, she was set up in the tent that Grandpa had built in the back yard. "Too bad ," Daddy added, "Helen cried when she told her first fortune and had to go home!" Lloyd Reutenbeck was painted all purple and yellow and planted in a cage where he paced back and forth and hollered a lot as "The Wild Man." The whole afternoon was successful – over three hundred people, including the professional circus performers, came! The circus folk enjoyed the performance so much that they gave all the kids tickets to their circus. This was Al Bell's first public appearance as an entertainer, and it certainly gave him the impetus to continue.

At the age of seven and a half, Al Bell was left in the world without his adoring mother. The young wife and mother, Maude Evelyn Robbins Bell, succumbed to anemia. As Daddy put it, "No one knew at that time that simply eating iron-rich liver would have saved her life." William Lloyd Bell gave blood for his wife time and time again, but to no avail. From a nearby hospital, she was moved to the upstairs in the doctor's home. Although she lay weak and languishing, she wrote many letters to her family in that florid long hand common to many writers of that day.

Daddy remembers that his Aunt Cora and her son came all the way from Boston to visit his mother in the hospital. They were city folks, and rarely, if ever, traveled as far west as Iowa. Little Allen Bell and his cousin were standing in the hospital room when suddenly, the boy from Boston pointed out the window, and with the most astonished look on his face, squeaked, "WHAT'S THAT??!"

Daddy, expecting some amazing sight to be outside, looked in the direction his cousin was pointing, and then answered calmly, "That's a horse."

When Grandma Bell died, Daddy's Aunt Grace and Uncle Ray came to live with the Bell family permanently. One vivid memory of Daddy's shortly after was of standing with his father inside their house on a dreary November day. They looked out the window and saw a robin perched on a wire near the barn.  Grandpa Bell watched the bird for a moment, and then sadly recited the poem:

> "The North Wind shall blow
> And we shall have snow
> And what will the Robin do then, poor thing?
>
> He'll hide in the barn
> With his head 'neath his wing.
> That's what he'll do then, poor thing."

My dad mentioned his mother frequently when I was growing up. He always had a picture of her on his dresser; she bore a wistful, melancholy expression. He used to tell my sister and me that we resembled her.  There is no doubt that Daddy's mother had surely been the mainstay in Grandpa Bell's life. According to Daddy, "She held her husband together and kept him going in one direction."  At this point, my dad's eyes would grow moist, and he would wipe away a tear or two.  Swallowing hard, because his own life became hard after her death, he would continue, "So, when she died, my dad just fell apart."

## Chapter Ten

After Grandma's early demise, the Bell clan, which now included Grace and Ray, made a trip to Denver, Colorado – a long, long ways in those days. Their plan was to sell their Grandfather's house. Great Grandpa Bell had lived in Sioux City where he had a big department store before moving to Denver. He had become "quite a well-made man, worth about fifty thousand dollars." Daddy was named for him. No one had bothered to worry about his house in Denver until Evelyn Bell died, but now they decided to get together and sell it. The group of Iowa travelers ventured west; Daddy recalled spending half a day stuck in the mud outside of Wahoo, Nebraska. Somehow they finally made it to Denver where they sold the house and returned to Iowa. They moved to Sioux City where Lloyd and Ray went into the sign painting business

Aunt Grace took care of the two boys, who had a difficult time adjusting to apartment living. They had an especially hard time being quiet. One day Allen, who was very bored and antsy, began pestering his aunt. "Can I play the piano?"

"Goodness, no!" she replied. "It's too noisy in an apartment house to play the piano."

"Well," he hesitated. "Can I, can I play with my ball?"

"Oh, no!" she cried.

"Can I sing?"

Exasperated, Aunt Grace gave a final "NO!"

Daddy stuck his hands in his pockets and thought for a minute. Then he whispered slyly, "Okay, Aunt Grace. Would you care if I sewed?"

The whole family eventually moved to a house on Grand Avenue.

It was a huge white house with three floors and a cupola on top. Allen and his brother Lloyd frequently went ice skating in Grand View Park. There were no shoe skates then, just runners that strapped over your shoes. They spent hours and hours, skating on their "ankles", and when their ankles finally gave out, they would trudge home, tired but happy. It was in Sioux City that Al Bell learned to ride a bike. He was eight or nine years old, and although bicycles were quite expensive, a very nice neighbor named "Zan" owned one. Zan was very generous and really wanted to help his friend, Allen, learn how to bike ride. Zan sat on the back fender with his feet near the ground while Daddy pumped and steered. Day after day, they'd ride that bike, Zan keeping the balance while Daddy pedaled and steered. One afternoon, Daddy turned around to say something to his friend on the back, and Zan was –gone! Al Bell was riding solo.

Daddy's Aunt Mame and her daughters, Lola and Evelyn, lived with the family for a brief period, and the family decided to move again to Clinton to live with Uncle Mose. In those days, all the roads were dirt, except for Lincoln Highway, the road that crossed the nation, and it was gravel. It was a good road except for when it rained, and then it was pretty bad. The group started out for Clinton early in the day, and about twenty or thirty miles outside Sioux City, they had to stop for gas. As Al Bell described the story, "Now, Uncle Ray considered himself to be quite an authority on driving; my father didn't understand much about cars, so there were few conflicts, except in this particular case. Upon leaving the gas station, Ray, rather than going on east towards Clinton, turned right around and headed back for Sioux City. Everyone in the car blurted out, 'Hey, Uncle Ray! Aren't you going the wrong way?' Uncle Ray was miffed that his driving abilities were being doubted and continued driving. My dad just sat there, silent, and stared out the window."

"After many miles of frustrated silence in the car, Uncle Ray mused, 'You know, Lloyd, I've seen some of these things before – just today.'"

"My father turned and said very quietly, 'Yeah, you've been going in the wrong direction.'"

It was a short stay in Clinton, too. The Bells lived in a red three story house from where the boys could look out and see the Mississippi River. The next move was to Rock Island on 18th Street and 30th Avenue. Their house was on a corner, diagonal from Grimm's grocery.

Uncle Ray kept saying, "We'll charge groceries for a year, and then we'll move." Aunt Grace would protest indignantly, but the very next week, he'd say the same thing. Daddy admitted that his uncle might very well have been serious, too.

It was in Rock Island that Daddy fell from a pile of poles where he'd been climbing and broke his arm. Aunt Grace prayed over his arm and then took him to the hospital where he was given gas, probably ether. A mask was placed over his face, and Daddy remembers this big yellow ball of light going around and around. Strangely enough, when he awoke, his arm was all set. Note: My sister remembers our dad telling her that, when he lived in Lost Nation, he broke his arm there, too. Apparently, when he tried to fly off the garage roof with an umbrella, the umbrella quickly collapsed.

In the summer, Al Bell used to go swimming in a culvert way out on 18th Avenue. This was about a mile and a half out of Rock Island, and this is where he became acquainted with the infamous Twelfth Street Gang. A toughie named Bud Headley ran his gang with an iron fist. In the beginning, little Allen (Daddy was small for his age) was an innocent little boy who was scared to go into the water. "Well, ol' Bud swaggered over to me. This was the first time we'd ever seen each other. He picked me up and threw me into the water, sneering 'Sink or Swim!' Of course, I swam no more than six or seven strokes out of the deep water, but I made it!" And that's how and where Al Bell first learned to swim. On the way home that day, as if further humiliation was necessary, he said, "I was breathing through my mouth as I always did, and I actually swallowed a fly! Is there anything more revolting?"

A few days after he'd broken his arm, which was still in a sling, one of Bud's gang stopped him just a block from home. Daddy told me, "He was kinda sassy to me, so I was sassy back to him. Then he demanded, 'Where're you goin?'"

"I answered, 'None of your business!'"

Al Bell played both of them animatedly. "'If you don't tell me where you're goin', I'll crack you one!'"

"'You crack me one and I'll crack you!' I retorted. And the first thing you know, with my broken right arm in a sling, I hit him left-handed, and then took off, faster than I thought I could run, in a circuitous route all the way home!"

In Long View Park, there was a wading pool which attracted

everybody on those unbearably hot and muggy summer days. Daddy remembers walking up to the pool on one of those humid afternoons to cool off, where a big fight was in progress. Bud and all of his gang were kicking all the "independents" out of the pool. They got Al Bell, too. Then as Daddy watched from a distance, Bud and his gang lords, celebrating their victory, sprawled and stretched out comfortably in the shallow pool, looking like the bullies they were.

There was another swimming pool, a real pool quite a ways from town where you had to pay a dime. One sultry day, Al Bell couldn't resist the temptation to spend a dime to go wading. Up on the shore, a tanned, muscular woman was instructing a class of girls in the fine art of the backstroke. Daddy, fascinated (with either the lesson or the girls), watched and listened as he unconsciously backed up and slipped into deeper water. The swimming teacher demonstrated the stroke with her arms. The girls hung on every word and gesture, and Daddy realized that he was now up to his chin in water. The bottom of the pool kept sliding under his feet, and as he stood there with the water fast approaching his mouth, he thought frantically, "I can't ask a woman to help me out of this pool – I'd rather drown!" And then he realized, "You ARE drowning, you fool!" He was fast going down. Without another thought, he screamed, "HELP, LADY!" whereupon the instructor turned abruptly to see a boy thrashing about in the pool. She raced over and smoothly rescued a very embarrassed Al Bell out of the deep end.

Daddy remarked that in those neighborhoods, you either had to belong to a gang or get killed. In this case, the choice was that of Bud's gang or a rival gang. Since Bud's was the closest and most powerful gang in the area, the Twelfth Street Gang seemed like the obvious choice. One day, one of Bud's henchmen wandered into the Bell yard, walked up to my then fifty-four pound father, and told him to report to Bud's house. It seemed that the gang had just met and decided they could use Allen as a messenger boy. He also was given the additional task of spying on other gangs.

The Bells lived on 18th and 30th for little more than a year. Daddy commented that he didn't know whether they ever paid Grimm's grocery or not. Their next move was to 28th and 8th Avenue. This was right across from the Lily sisters who ran the beer brewery. The Lily sisters had quite an impressive house, and the Bell brothers used to sit on their steps and wonder who owned the big, shiny cars that drove in and out across the street.

The family consisted of Grace and Ray again. Uncle Ray and his brother Lloyd sold Maytag and Speedqueen washers. Uncle Ray, the eccentric, always wanted to paint a huge sign with a giant pair of scissors drawn on, stating "WE CUT THE PRICE." Years later, when they tried their luck at selling washers again, he made the sign.

A German immigrant family lived right next door, and they had a daughter named Lisa. She was about the same age as Allen and his brother, and the three of them played together frequently. When Lisa's parents called her in for supper, they would shout in German, of course, which sounded frightening to the boys. "Lisa," Daddy would quaver, "Are they mad at you?"

"No, Silly," she would reply. "They just want me to come in to eat!" (It's ironic that Al Bell chose to be a German major in college, and that he used the language easily many years later for their travels in Europe.) Lisa was Al Bell's first girlfriend. To impress her, Daddy would borrow the only bicycle in the neighborhood and take her riding. "She sat on the handlebars so daintily and pretty," Daddy described. "I finally decided one day that I just had to kiss her. I gathered my courage as I peddled, and I began leaning toward her, closer and closer, until I lurched forward, and 'Smack!' got my lips right on her cheek. I nearly dumped the bike, I was so delighted." Daddy added, "She wasn't nearly as impressed as I was!"

Down the street and around the corner was a little grocery store run by an Italian family. Tony, their son, was in Al Bell's class at school, and they became fairly good friends. Daddy recalled the night he was invited to eat at Tony's house. Tony drank wine along with the rest of the family, but when Al Bell was offered a glass, he refused, thinking it couldn't possibly be the right thing to do.

Behind the Bell house was a birdhouse perched on top of the double garage. Daddy reminisced, "The birdhouse was meant to be for respectable martins, but unfortunately, a big nest of mean old hornets lived in it instead. I had always imagined myself as a sort of Sir Lancelot or Don Quixote – a brave hero brandishing a gleaming long sword. So, one particularly dull afternoon, I found a big stick for my sword, and I crawled on the roof of the garage and began warfare with the hornets. BZZZZ, BZZZZ, BZZZZZZ! They weren't at all happy about being rousted out of their comfortable home. They dive bombed their attacker – me – and circled and dived again while I fought heroically and shouted, 'GET OUT OF THIS BIRDHOUSE! GO AWAY!!' All the time I was swirling my sword around and wildly poking, stabbing inside the birdhouse. For FORTY-FIVE minutes, I battled those nasty hornets until, finally, they left. The war was over. I WON!" But Al Bell had so many stings that Aunt Grace had to soak almost his entire body with baking soda and water. What a price to pay! I wonder if those martins appreciated their "Knight in Swollen Armor"?

The Bell brothers never meant to invite trouble, but trouble they wreaked when there was nothing to do, and they always invented things to do. One morning, Aunt Grace had gone shopping. Allen and Lloyd were alone…bored…restless. They wandered down to the basement, and lo and behold! They discovered a pile of clothes that appeared to be in need of washing. "I know!" piped up eleven year-old Allen. "Let's help out Aunt Grace by washing these dirty clothes for her!" Lloyd agreed that this was a good idea. So, they threw the colored socks and old pajamas and ladies' undergarments all into the tub, then through the wringer, and proudly hung up the whole bunch on the clothesline. Shortly after they were finished and stood admiring their work, Grace returned home.

"Guess what we did for you, Aunt Grace? We washed all those clothes down in the basement!"

Aunt Grace stared at them. "You did what?"

"Look, we even hung them up on the line. Aren't we good boys?" She threw her hands up in the air and moaned, as she looked out to see her old throwaways and ragged underwear ready for the ragbag, blowing gently in the breeze for all the world to see. Daddy admitted, "We were quite a disgrace to the family for a while."

By this time, the boys were old enough to go downtown to the Saturday afternoon movies. And they LOVED to go to the movies. It didn't take them long to devise a foolproof method to ensure that they could go every week. On Saturday after lunch, Uncle Ray would lie on the sofa and read the paper. Lloyd and Allen would begin wrestling with each other, pushing, squealing, and generally making a nuisance of themselves, right by Uncle Ray. After a few minutes of the boys' boisterous play, Uncle Ray would put the paper over his face to avoid the commotion. They'd keep it up, fighting and throwing each other down, until finally, in Al Bell's words, "We'd driven Uncle Ray right up the wall!"

At which point, Ray would put down the paper, and announce, "Hey! You boys! I'll give you a dime to go to the movie, if you promise to stay for both shows." The wrestling immediately ceased. Daddy continued, "We would jump up, grab our dimes and take off. It worked every Saturday!"

As Daddy told the story, "One typical afternoon, after we boys had procured our movie money, we started off to see 'The Girl of the Golden West.' Aunt Grace had picked it out as the nicest movie showing, plus it had cowboys in it. After we got downtown, however, we looked across the street, and we saw that 'Phantom of the Opera' was playing with that scary Lon Chaney as the Phantom. We stood and looked at that marquee for a long time, squirming in our shoes, knowing that we were supposed to see 'The Golden Girl of the West.' We stood and looked from one side of the street to the other, our eyes always darting back to the 'Phantom' and staying there." Al Bell smiled wistfully as he continued, "We stood and stood and then looked at each just long enough to decide. Sneaking furtively across the street, we paid our dimes to see Lon Chaney as the terrible Phantom. Creeping inside, making sure we weren't seen, we found our seats just as the organist began the spooky music which was to continue through the entire picture. Eyes glazed, mouths hanging open, we clung to the arms of our chairs – speechless."

Obviously, the two youngsters were duly impressed with the scary movie. Daddy concluded, "We shivered upon re-entering the outside world, and then we ran all the way home, too terrified to look back. What was worse – we couldn't tell anyone what we'd just experienced! Somehow, we kept our fear under control until bedtime, and then going upstairs, we jumped under the covers and hugged each other tight all night."

The Bell boys were a superstitious, easily spooked pair of youngsters. In this house, their bedroom was next to the attic. Especially when their folks were gone, they could hear a terrible clanking, clanking in that room which, incidentally, was all boarded up. They would shiver, pull the covers over their heads, and whisper that it was probably a ghostly skeleton which was locked in there long ago.

It was here in Rock Island that Al Bell learned to ski, or rather tried to ski. The Patten boys, friends of the Bell brothers, lived right in back of Grandview Park. There was a "jump-off place", two or three feet high, and the boys would ski, jump off, fall down, ski again and fall down. Some of Daddy's worst moments about that time were of trying to sell magazines: *The Ladies Home Journal, The Saturday Evening Post, The Country Gentlemen* and others. Daddy certainly learned the art of selling as he matured; Mother used to say that he could sell ice to Eskimos.

The finale to Daddy's time in Rock Island was the Marble Tournament, sponsored by the YMCA downtown. Local contests were held all over the city, and Al Bell won that first competition fairly easily. Then came the semi-division which he also won. Daddy commented that "the boy who could have beaten me came down with a good case of the mumps right before the contest." He continued, "On a Saturday night, right downtown, the Finals were held in front of a crowd of people. The game was close all the way through; the other finalist and I played as though we weren't even being watched. My competitor, the best marble player in the area, was being cheered on by his friends, when all of a sudden, he knocked his marble out of the ring. His shooter was still inside the ring, ready for me to shoot it and become the winner."

Al Bell remembers the voices yelling, "Don't hit it! Don't hit it!" and they screamed, "You can't hit it out! If you hit it out, you'll be the new champion and he's the best!" Trying desperately to ignore the crowd, Daddy got down on one knee and looked over the situation. Then, WHAP! He'd shot his opponent's shooter out of the ring, and Al Bell became the Marble Champ of Rock Island.

It's natural for youngsters to become so consumed with their own lives that they become unaware of external happenings. It seems that, unbeknownst to the Bell brothers, their father had become re-acquainted with a lady from Lost Nation. The first thing the boys knew, they were being introduced to their new mother, Beulah Gable. It was moving time again, too.

The family left Rock Island and moved to 30th and Harrison in Davenport. They lived in an upstairs apartment over Jasper Grocery, and Daddy went to J. B. Young, Jr. High School with about eight or nine hundred other adolescents. He claimed to have had three girlfriends simultaneously, but he admits, "I kept 'em separated!" After school one day, Al Bell walked across the block to play baseball, as he usually did, but on this particular afternoon, right in the middle of the fun, he caught the ball with the tip of his little finger. When you catch a baseball like that, as most of us know, it can really hurt. Daddy's finger swelled up, and he couldn't sleep at all that night. About three o'clock in the morning, a little old lady knocked at the Bells' front door.

"I've heard you walking all night. What's the problem?" Daddy showed her his finger, and she promptly demanded, "Get a pan of hot water, and sit down with me at the table." While he soaked his swollen finger, the two of them talked and talked.

About an hour later, Daddy looked at her, surprised, and commented, "It quit hurting." She said goodnight, and he crawled into bed and went right to sleep. My father was always drawn to elderly ladies; having lost his mother at such an early age, he may have been searching for a replacement. In every church he ever attended, he had a fan club of little old ladies, and he charmed every one of them.

Like many ambitious youngsters, Daddy had a paper route in Davenport. He delivered *The Daily Democrat*, one hundred fifteen papers on his first route. With time, Al Bell earned enough money to buy his first bicycle. On Saturday nights he would be found, sitting and folding papers with the other boys. He remembered one lady who always gave him a piece of pie when he came by to collect. Eventually, he did so well that he was asked if he wanted to deliver the Sunday paper. Daddy began at five a.m. on Sundays, and his route, which included one hundred fifteen papers in just one large apartment building, took until noon.

Every Saturday, the Bell boys went swimming at Duck Creek, which Daddy informed me is a golf course now. One afternoon, Allen just couldn't resist the temptation to show off a spectacular dive. "This is gonna be a Dead Stick dive!" he bragged. High up in the air he jumped, and SPLASH! But because the water was only five feet deep, Al Bell hit his head on the bottom and snapped his front tooth right off, leaving it at the bottom of Duck Creek. My dad used to do a "jack knife" off the end of the dock at our farm pond, and it was an amazingly high, clean dive. Mother used to worry that the pond wasn't deep enough. In fact, it was filling up with the neighbor's eroded silt as years passed, but Daddy had learned a hard lesson at Duck Creek. At home and later at Lake Okoboji, he always surfaced quickly, grinning that mischievous smile that recalled a young boy's triumph.

NOTE: My sister Rhea recently told me that she remembers clearly the day when she was three or four that Daddy broke his nose diving in the shallow end of the a pool. "I can still see it," she said. "It was about two feet deep." They were living on the Mississippi backwater then. "Mother told him not to…"

During this time, Grandpa Bell had worked his way up to supervisor for Speed Queen washing machines. This was a job that dealt with traveling to different areas and teaching salesmen how to sell. "Well," my dad explained, "he got to wandering around the country, and then just plain disappeared. Our new stepmother wrote letters to our mother's family, as she didn't know of any of my dad's relatives around. Finally, Great Grandpa Robbins wrote that it was fine if she sent us to Washburn, Illinois where he lived. Relieved, Beulah put Lloyd Junior and me on a train, and we never saw her again."

## Chapter Eleven

The porters on the train were very nice to the twelve and ten year-old boys. They arrived in La Rose, Illinois about ten o'clock at night, where their Uncle Ed's son, Will and his wife picked them up in their Model-T Ford. It was thirty miles an hour all the way to their grandpa's house. "Grandpa Robbins was about eighty years old then, and he was pretty weak." Daddy recalled sitting on his grandpa's bed every morning where they would talk and talk. Once, Great Grandpa let Allen hook his three buckle shoes which was quite a time-consuming event.

Daddy remembers a tool house and hog house that stood out in the back. In fact, he had the startling experience of witnessing the hog house blow up because a sow had eaten a stick of dynamite! One afternoon, the boys were playing in the back of the barn when they saw Uncle Ed come out of the house. They watched as he cautiously looked all around before stepping into the barn. Peeking out from their hiding place, Lloyd and Allen saw their uncle take a bottle out of the hay in the manger, look once more over his shoulder, and then take a big swig. He wiped his mouth with his sleeve, hid the bottle very carefully back in the hay, and then walked casually back into the house. Mystified, the two boys waited for a moment, and then crept up to the manger. After digging out the bottle, they too, looked around to see if anyone was watching. They quietly removed the cap and each took a whiff of the contents. "Whew! That smells awful!" whispered Lloyd, and Allen deduced that this must be some kind of liquor. They tucked the evil bottle back into Uncle Ed's hiding place, and swore off drinking until a later date in their futures.

Half a mile south of Great Grandpa's house was the place

where Daddy's mother was buried. Many years later, Daddy buried his father beside her. Al Bell attended country school here for about three months. It was a one room schoolhouse with eight grades, and Daddy remembers having a total of four in his class. In later years, my mother taught at a country school whose students produced many tears and much laughter in my parents' lives. However, we'll save that for a later chapter. Overall, both memories must have been a good experience, as my parents enthusiastically enrolled me in country school when we moved to rural Menlo. Daddy loved the potlucks, programs and fellowship in that little school, as well.

Allen and his brother Lloyd were, by this time, becoming fairly used to being shuffled around from relative to relative. When they left their Grandpa Robbins' house, Daddy felt that it was because their grandpa wasn't very well. And he did die shortly thereafter. Daddy said that it was probably a train that took them to Kansas because "Everybody went by train in those days. Cars weren't the most dependable things in the world," he added.

Uncle Tom Robbins, Evelyn Bell's brother, drove to Lawrence to pick up his nephews. He brought them to his house outside Oskaloosa, Kansas. Allen and Lloyd lived with Uncle Tom and his family for about two years on "the poorest eighty acres you've ever seen." The boys' new family consisted of Uncle Tom and his wife Ina, Donald who was sixteen, Lawrence, nicknamed "Bud", who was fifteen, and Evelyn, twelve. "These were BIG people in size," Daddy chuckled. "Evelyn was sixty inches around in the eighth grade."

The house was an unpainted shack. A washing machine stood on the porch outside. "This was the kind of primitive washer with a handle that I had to push back and forth, thus moving the agitator." The Bell brothers were moved into the northwest room, the coldest room in the house. In the winter, the boys wore long johns and socks to bed, and still hugged each other all night to keep from freezing. "The wind blew through the cracks of that rundown old house," Daddy remembered. "Many mornings, we woke up to find snow on the covers." He and Lloyd would leap out of bed, run downstairs, and dress in front of the stove to get ready for school.

The outhouse, or privy, was out back. Baths were taken in a washtub in front of the stove while Aunt Ina supervised. In the very beginning of their stay, Allen and Lloyd were considered to be guests, "but all that changed immensely." Daddy asked one day if he could give hay to the horses, King and Queen. "Well…" they hesitated, "all right." Two days later, if Daddy missed haying the horses, he was demoted to milking the cows, feeding the hogs, and dragging home one hundred pound bags of bran from the mill. Daddy commented dryly that, "My back troubles all stem from carrying hundred pound sacks when I was only ninety-eight pounds myself."

Al Bell had no sooner volunteered to do chores, than he was regularly milking three cows morning and night, which meant that he had to get up at five a.m. When he began helping by pumping water for the cows and horses, he remembers one frosty morning Donald persuaded his younger cousin Allen into sticking his tongue on the pump handle! (See the film, "A Christmas Story" for a graphic depiction of this act.) Thirty minutes later, Daddy, having no other option or help, had to tear off skin to get his tongue loose. In addition to the pain, was the embarrassment of being duped by Donald.

"Everyone's destined to do something," Daddy mused, as he recalled working in the hayloft during haying. "I've always had to work up in the hayloft!" That first time was probably the worst, as it was a muggy ninety degrees outside, and one hundred ten inside the dusty, scratchy barn. (Many of us have had similar experiences, and Al Bell didn't spare his own children from that miserable chore, either.)

The next summer, my dad learned to drive King and Queen. He did his first farming that summer, too, with a one row cultivator pulled behind the team. There was no such thing as contour plowing in those pre-Dust Bowl days and Al simply planted straight up and down the hills. After school and on Saturdays, Daddy remembered picking cockleburs. "It was awful hot in Kansas," he recalled. "We'd go up and down those rows, and I'd think of all the injustices we had to bear, and then I'd declare that we were going to run away by the end of the row. But we'd get hungry and decide that maybe we ought to leave after dinner."

The family radio lured them to stay after dinner. "We used to listen to Jenny Wren station from Lawrence, Kansas. They'd say, 'W-R-E-N Radio. And every Saturday night, we'd listen to hillbilly music with Uncle Ezry."

Life was hard in Kansas. "We were so poor that we ate pancakes and gravy with sowbelly. We rarely had real meat. But I remember that fresh carrots out of the garden, which I had hated before, were the best tasting carrots of my life. We had gone a long time without vegetables."

"The Perrys lived nearby. He was a 'book farmer.' They had a nice house, nice car, painted buildings. He gave me my first paying job – picking strawberries for three cents a quart. The only time I had to earn money was between 3:30 and 5:30 a.m. because Uncle Tom had me working all the rest of the time."

"On Saturdays, after our chores were done, late afternoon or so, the whole family piled in their old Dodge, and we went into Oskaloosa for Saturday night. I always took my little brother to the show to see the cowboys. We'd see four shows for ten cents a piece. In fact, Lloyd still owes me forty cents!"

"We walked to school three miles away. In good weather, it wasn't bad. In bad weather, it was terrible! We took sandwiches which were always frozen in the winter because we had to keep them in the coat closet which wasn't heated. Mr. Gregg was our teacher. I fell in love with his beautiful daughter, Naomi. The Gibbs girls lived just a half mile north of the schoolhouse. They were nice. We kids would square dance and sing in the light of the barnyard while the old folks sat in the house and talked."

"My best friend was Frankie Ellers. Some Saturdays, I got to go to his house. We'd go up in the hayloft in the barn and Frankie would act out cowboy movies that I hadn't seen." Daddy paused. "Frankie was killed in college. He was hitch hiking, something a lot of us guys did to get from town to the campus. Well, the cars wouldn't stop to pick up Frankie. He finally decided to lie down on the road. Surely, they'd have to stop. A car ran over him and killed him."

"Some Saturdays when there was a lot of snow, Donald and Bud took their guns and went out rabbit hunting. We were too young. The sun would shine on the snow, and the rabbits would pop up. WHAM! They'd shoot rabbits, and we'd run pick them up and put them in a pile. Once they shot about twenty rabbits while they just sat on a hill."

"The last fall I lived there, Donald, Bud, Evelyn and I drove a '23 Dodge into Oskaloosa to high school. It was our freshman year. We'd missed freshman initiation, due to working on the farm. Anyway, at noon, we'd roar into the country to eat our sack lunches, and then just barely make it back in time for our one o'clock class. Well, everybody had been initiated but us, so one day, we tore out of school at noon, jumped into the old Dodge, and there was a car three blocks down the street that was waiting for us. Donald, who was driving of course, immediately ducked through an alley and came out on another street. Sure enough, another car was waiting at the corner. Donald headed back toward town. They had every side road blocked; they got us to the square and stopped us. Then they tore us out of the car and pulled us to a side street off the square. While they held us, they made a double line half a block long. All the boys had sticks, broken boards and whips. One at a time, they made us run the 'gauntlet'. I didn't weigh over a hundred pounds, but only Bud and I made it to the other end. The other two were knocked down, screaming and 'paddled out'. I don't know how I ever made it. I couldn't feel a thing after the first three guys hit me. Needless to say, we didn't go to school for the rest of the day."

"One day when it was really snowing hard, we got out of school early. The roads weren't good anyway because they were dirt, and we lived about seven miles from school. The snow was blowing so hard that you couldn't tell the narrow road from the ditches. Donald did his best, but we soon got stuck in a snowdrift. The old radiator boiled while we rocked the car back and forth. Finally, we gave up and all four of us walked home – about four miles. We couldn't see a thing, so we just stayed between the fences. It was after dark when we got home. Uncle Tom and Aunt Ina really didn't expect us; they thought we'd be frozen."

For lack of anything else to do, Donald and Bud picked on the "little boys". They would chase Allen and Lloyd all over the farm, catch them, and then beat them up. If they caught Lloyd first, who was, of course, younger, Daddy would jump on them until Lloyd pried himself loose and could hide, and then Daddy took the beating. He was very protective of his brother who actually grew up to be the larger of the two.

Whenever my dad told us kids of his Kansas memories, we always felt sad, thinking of the abuse that he and his brother suffered at the hands of their cousins, not to mention the hard conditions under which they lived. This was their lot simply because of their young mother's premature death, and her husband's failure to cope with his own sorrow.

## Chapter Twelve

After nearly two years in Kansas, the Bell boys received a letter from Morrison, Illinois. For two little boys who'd never received a personal letter before, they were quite impressed. It was addressed to Masters Allen and Lloyd Bell, in care of Tom Robbins, Oskaloosa, Kansas. "The letter was from my father who had suddenly regained his memory." Daddy explained, "It seems that he'd been down in Arkansas, helping some friend paint a movie screen, and fell off a scaffold. He hurt his back and head, but he regained his memory. My dad had returned to Aunt Grace and Uncle Ray's where Ray had been the stationmaster of the railroad in Morrison, Illinois. He and Uncle Ray went back to selling Speed Queen and Maytag washers."

"Aunt Grace's daughter, Gladys, lived in Morrison, too. Her husband, Glen Smith, had a clothing store there. He made me my first pair of long pants. I wore them to college, too, complete with pleats in the front and nine-inch cuffs. Uncle Ray was an antique nut. He was crazy about Jenny Lind beds, so he'd buy them cheap, and I sanded them down for ten cents an hour. Talk about a boring, tiring job! I earned money in Morrison by sanding beds and mowing lawns. Aunt Gladys had the biggest lawn I'd ever seen. Her yard was a quarter of a block! Once, she paid me a whole dollar!"

"Being a Christian Scientist, Aunt Grace was a great believer in faith healing. I remember one time she had a great big tub of hot water on the stove. Somehow, she pulled that tub off the stove, accidentally, and scalded herself. She never said a word, even though I saw boiling water pour all over her body. Gladys tried to get her to go to the doctor, but Grace refused. She just put salve on herself and prayed. We were dumbfounded."

Al Bell's passion for golf began around this time. Frank Donovan was a professional golfer in Morrison. Daddy explained, "There were three classes of caddies: 'C' class was the beginner who earned twenty-five cents a round after six months. 'B' class meant you got thirty-five cents after working for a year, and to become 'A' class you had to take a test with Frank, caddying for him. If he liked you, you could charge fifty cents a round. While we waited for an opportunity to caddy, we boys would sit around, shaking Coke bottles, then aim the fizz at each other."

"Finally, I got my chance to be an 'A' class. Things started out all right except for the fact that Frank had been drinking. The first hole went fine with a nice, long, high start. The ball landed on the lush, flat driveway. On the second hole, the ball was short. The third hole had woods on each side. Well, Frank sliced into the woods. He was so mad that he threw his driver into the woods after the ball! There we were, me in the middle of my first round of caddying for the professional golfer who had been drinking too much. He was mad as hops. It looked like I'd never make it to 'A' class. Luckily, when I went into the woods, I found his ball and his club. Frank never said a word, but I passed."

Daddy joined Boy Scouts (and eventually became an Eagle Scout.) He explained that Uncle Ray had a Model-A with a rumble seat. "One time, he let me drive it. I took my whole patrol, seven other boys and myself, out on a campout. Once we were there, the car wouldn't go forward up a hill, so I coasted back down, put it in reverse, and backed up the hill!" (Many cars had gravity-fed gas tanks in those long ago days before fuel pumps were invented. The scary part was that the gasoline tank was in the dashboard.)

"Aunt Grace was rather heavy. She had a stroke, and I was the only one home. She was down in the basement washing clothes, and I heard her kind of holler, so I ran downstairs. She had collapsed and was lying on the floor. As large as she was, I don't know how I did it, but somehow, I picked her up. The good Lord was with me. I carried her upstairs to the bedroom and put her on the bed."

"That summer, my dad got a job in Prophetstown, Illinois which was named for a famous Indian prophet and was then known for the Eclipse Lawn Mower Factory. He worked as a salesman at the International Harvester Implement company for thirty-five dollars a week, plus commission." (My Uncle Bill – Lloyd – worked for International many years later.) "Of course, we moved to Prophetstown. I took my first piano lesson from Mr. Vincent who was real nice. I tried and tried – do re mi, do re mi...until I went out of my mind. I was spending my own money! I finally gave up after three lessons, but continued to teach myself." (Al Bell's persistence and determination to play the piano paid off. He played beautifully by ear, for the rest of his life.)

Daddy enrolled in high school in Prophetstown where he continued his freshman year. "When I walked into the assembly hall that first day of school, I must have looked pretty funny. The girls giggled at me, and some of the boys snickered. When I look back at a freshman picture, I can see why. I was in the back of the science room, standing on a chair because I was kinda little, and I had a short, funny haircut – no wax or oil, the water had disappeared, and it was standing straight up."

Trigonometry was very confusing. "I was supposed to estimate the height of a tree with a pencil; I never did understand. One day in assembly, while I was studying something, I began playing with a straight pin that I'd found. I'd stick it in my thumb and flip it up and down. I'd read, flip it up and down, and read again. I was sticking it in my thumb further, and then I'd read some more. Next thing I knew, the pin was gone from my thumb and in my mouth! I tried to cough and spit it up, but the thing had completely disappeared. I never did figure out where the pin went, but I assume I must have swallowed it. I must still have it in me!"

Al Bell's most embarrassing moment happened in that assembly hall. "There was a fellow who'd come to school once in a while to entertain. He played guitar and sang current popular songs. After he'd sung quite a few that I didn't know very well, he asked if there were any requests. Several others asked for songs, and then I raised my hand, and asked very seriously, if the singer would please sing 'Letter Edged in Black'. It was a very sad, potent song that always reminded me of my mother's death, but it was definitely out of fashion by then. Well, the other kids just pounded their desks and screamed in hysteria as if I'd just arrived from the hills of Kansas." Oh, the cruelty of adolescence.

After the Bells had lived in Prophetstown for a while, they moved to the south side of town to a square, two story white house. It was at the edge of town, next to Paul Blair's father's filling station. Mr. Blair was also the Pontiac dealer in town. "A couple of sisters, old maids, lived nearby, and they let me practice on their piano after school. They had a hard coal stove, my first exposure to one, that was toasty warm. Bright crackles would be coming out of the Isinglass windows of the stove. That stove burned nearly twenty-four hours without refueling or shaking down ashes. The sisters lived right across the street from a barefoot Belgian lady who had a whole bunch of kids. She did our washing. She was always screaming at her daughter-in-law."

"There was a pear orchard in back of the house we lived in, and a square little old shed where I raised banty (Bantam) chickens. I made wine in the attic of that shed. I'd buy canned peaches and apricots and sugar, and then my father would complain: 'The groceries are costing a dollar a day. I can't afford to keep you kids.' And I'd keep making wine in crocks, and it would turn out to be apricot and peach vinegar! Once I raised brown New Zealand rabbits, but they'd eat their young, and I couldn't afford to keep them any more."

"At thirteen, I was buying the groceries and cooking the meals. Aunt Grace had taught me a few things about cooking. I used to cook supper for my dad and brother – meat, potatoes and a vegetable. While it was getting ready, I'd have the little laundry stove in the corner of the kitchen red hot, and I'd have a pan of oatmeal or rice cooking over there. I'd be reading and getting culture clear up to my ears while dinner was cooking, and I'd be eating oatmeal or rice."

"Once when I was in the grocery store, probably getting more peaches and apricots, a little boy was there shopping, too. The grocery store owner asked him, 'Say, didn't you have another baby at your house yesterday morning?'"

'Yup.'

'What're you going to do for places for them to sleep and sit at the same table? What're you going to do with them at night?'

'Well, Pa says we're gonna pile 'em up like cordwood in the corners.'"

Daddy's first real buddy in Prophetstown was Curtis Hammond. "We'd been reading *The Last of the Mohicans*, and decided if they could do it, so could we. So, he and I struck out along the river, going north out of town, in just shorts and shirts – and no matches."

He was tall, red-haired and skinny; I was little, not red-haired and skinny. We built fires by rubbing sticks together, just like they taught us in Boy Scouts. But we had an awful time finding anything to eat. Finally, we ran a farmer's chicken down. We pulled all its feathers out, took our knife and cut its insides out, and cooked it over the fire. It was pretty smoky and pretty terrible, too. We kind of existed like that for three days, and finally decided that maybe things weren't so bad back home."

"Another time, we went clear up the Rock River and swiped some watermelons from an island out in the middle of the river. We crawled to the watermelons, so we wouldn't be seen, and then floated them out in the water. While they were floating, we stripped to our shorts. Then we swam underwater as long as we could with those melons bobbing up and down above us, and when we came up, the owner of those melons was shooting at us with a shotgun! We ducked underwater again, and swam as far as we could down river before we came up. The farmer had given up, so we caught up with our watermelons, herded them to the left bank, and took some home." Daddy continued, "The place where we left the watermelons was the city dump for Prophetstown. We used to go down on Saturdays and shoot rats. Talk about pollution!"

"Billy Matthews was a little younger than I; we called his sister Georgianne, 'Pud.' At night, we'd walk down the river to the car bridge. We could see the lights from town. On moonlit nights, we'd sit on the edge of the bridge over the river and sing 'Ol' Man River'."

"It was here that I started my photography. My brother, Lloyd had gotten an Eastman Kodak camera worth two dollars. About a block from our house, we had to cross the railroad track on the way to school. Well, I'd take that camera and follow the track out of town. I took pictures of flowers and trees, and once I got a picture of a groundhog that came out of his hole to see me. He was three or four feet away! I'd cross the bridge on the railroad trestles, and one day I noticed a little cabin down underneath the trees by the bridge. I met the people who lived there – old folks – and we got along real well. They'd give me a glass of milk or something, and then I'd start back home. Their radio would be on sometimes, and one night at sunset, as I crossed the bridge, I heard 'Cabin in the Cotton.' Whenever I heard that song from then on, it always reminded me of that little house by the bridge and walking back home in the evening sun."

"My brother and I had separate rooms upstairs in that house. One time, I got an incubator from someplace that held fifty to one hundred eggs. I used it as a bank. I painted it all up and put a cloth across the top, so it looked just like a little table. Well, my brother broke into my incubator by taking the hinges off, and he took sixteen half dollars that I'd saved. Then he and a friend bought a white raccoon, of all the dumb things to do. I told my dad about him taking my money and buying a white raccoon, but after he left for work, my brother got so mad at me for telling, that he chased me all over the house. I got in my room, shut the door and locked it. Then he took a big baseball bat and broke down two slats from the door. I just opened the window and dropped down to the ground. I went next door to the gas station and said, 'Say, my brother's kinda mad at me. Would anybody care if I hid upstairs in the attic for a while?' After a half hour or so, I heard a soft voice say, 'Has my brother been around here?' Then I knew he was over his 'mad', and it was safe to come down."

Al Bell reminisced about assorted memories from Prophetstown: It was here that he learned to play a popular Belgian game called Roly-Boly. He remembered that everyone would listen to the Chicago Cubs' games at Hunts' gas station. He added that he was still a Cubs fan because of that. At night, Daddy used to walk through the streets of Prophetstown which made his father wonder why he was wandering in the dark. "The lights hurt my eyes," Daddy explained, "so my dad bought me a pair of fifteen dollar glasses." He added that his prescription didn't change for many years after that.

During his junior year, Paul Blair, Marvin Hunt, Ryland Smith and Al Bell started a quartet for a school program. "Paul sang second tenor, Ryland was first tenor, we got Marvin to sing baritone, and I sang bass. After the program, we decided we'd start singing quartet numbers, but Marvin was having problems remembering the arrangements and getting enough time from his dad's filling station to practice, so he left the group, and we became a trio. We'd sit in cars or on corners, or go out riding, and we'd practice trio numbers. I can't remember anymore what they were, but we entered all the amateur contests all over that part of Illinois. We battled four year-old girls with blonde curly hair in red and pink dancing costumes who threatened to win over us, so we decided to quit as amateurs and went into it professionally."

"One night, I was the guest of Bob Romans who lived across from Hunts' station. We got ready to go to bed, and I noticed that were no pillows; I surmised these were poor people. I about broke my neck, sleeping on the flat mattress. Not until years later, did I find out that Belgians sleep without pillows!"

In the spring Al Bell picked strawberries for three cents a box every morning across the street at Sadie Mott's. He invented his own alarm clock by tying a string to his big toe, dropping it out the window where it came down about four feet from the ground, and around four a.m., Herb Mott would come over and jerk the string!

It was here that Daddy met Ted and Matt Lindberg and their family. Their father was a tool and die maker at Eclipse Lawn Mower Company. Daddy recalled, "He made four hundred dollars a month, regardless of good or bad times." He went on to say, "Ted and I became very good friends in high school. I used to go over and sit on his porch, and we'd talk about our dreams and aspirations. One day, I offered him a cigarette. This was back in the days when I thought smoking was smart," he added. "Ted looked at me for a minute and then asked, 'Would you care if I smoked it a little later on when I don't have anything to do? I'd just like to talk to you now.' So I gave him the cigarette. After dinner, we went up to his room, and after we'd talked for a while, Ted went over to a big box. He opened it up, and it was full of cigarettes! He'd been collecting them from the other boys, but he'd never smoked any of them. He said, 'Would you like a cigarette, Al?' Well, I didn't have much choice, so I took one."

"We used to have poker parties at my house because my dad was gone a lot at night. He worked at collecting and selling tractors and things. We would sit in the front room with the curtains up and just the ceiling light on. We'd drink some of my grape or orange or peach wine that I'd made in the attic of the chicken house. The wine was more like vinegar because I didn't know about capping the crocks. The neighbors would complain that we boys were gambling, because after drinking, we'd holler, betting money that the girls from bookkeeping class had given us. We'd sit there and bet fifteen, twenty thousand dollars. Well, the neighbors called the police, and the first thing you knew, a police car would pull up; we'd put the bookkeeping money away and just play with poker cards."

"Right behind our little house on the south side of town, to the right of the chicken house, I built a horseshoe pit. Tud Lindberg and I would practice and practice every afternoon after school. Eventually we got so good that we were the Horseshoe Champions of the school. In fact, I was the champion, and Tud was second place champion. We had lots of matches with other schools, and the last year of high school, we received our letter in Horseshoes!"

"Mr. Norman was a pretty strict sort of a superintendent. I remember there was a trial at school one time. Some boys had done something—taken a car or something – and my brother Lloyd was in the bunch. It was a big trial right in front of the assembly hall with lawyers, a judge and a jury. They were getting right down to my brother being a witness, when my father (who had come to school for this) told Mr. Norman that he'd 'change his face' if he didn't drop the whole trial! Mr. Norman dropped the trial."

"My dad was still selling implements for International Harvester, and it was a high-pressure business. My dad got high blood pressure and nerves; besides that, he was staying out late talking to farmers and pushing cars out of the mud. He finally wound up having to sleep half a day, or maybe two days in bed, just to get his blood pressure down and get his strength back. He just drove himself right through the Depression. He was an expert in selling, though. There aren't many people who can sell you a tractor, and then come back as a bill collector, and they still like you when they're done paying you for it!"

Al Bell playing guitar and singing his 'hill-billy' songs, circa 1932.

Al Bell played "my best basketball at Prophetstown High School" but had to settle for being on the second team. "I really didn't have a chance. I was kind of a skinny little runt. Two of the boys on first team turned out to be Olympic material – one as a pole vaulter, and the other throwing the javelin. I did play left field baseball, though, and earned my letter. The principal was the baseball coach, and once I threw a ball toward home, and it hit him in the calf. He got a charley horse and said some awful mean things under his breath."

"After an event at high school, we kids would go down to the Coke shop or down to the restaurant, and we'd sit and talk until probably eleven o'clock and then go home. I remember a girl by the name of Maude Brown who was 'one of the fellows', very popular with everybody. She and I used to talk a lot after the shows and games. I remember one night when we pledged to meet each other in that very same restaurant at the same table in thirty years. Somehow we never got around to it. My brother used to work at the Coke shop. We called him a Coke 'fiend' because he drank ten to fifteen Cokes a day, working behind the counter."

"I joined Boy Scout work when I lived in Prophetstown. I went from Tenderfoot to Eagle Scout. I was very, very proud because I was the first Eagle Scout in the county. I loved getting merit badges by cooking, camping, bicycling and astronomy. One time, we went cycling clear to Sterling which is eighteen miles, and then we came back which made thirty-six miles. So, we went out to the country and rode about six miles, which made our fifty miles of bicycling." Daddy added, "Kids today talk about driving fast. Well, my dad used to say, 'I don't want to be on the road. I want to be in Rock Island. I want to be in Prophetstown.' He drove one hundred miles an hour to get there, back in those days of 1933."

"I went to church very little in Prophetstown. There was nobody to take, or urge me to go, or tell me why I should go. One time, a buddy of mine named Lloyd Simister, whose father was the Methodist minister in town, took me to church. Well, I watched all the bad folks in town – the drinkers, the gamblers, the bad women – crawl up there on their knees and swear off all their iniquities, and say they'd never do them again. In a couple weeks' time, they were back to their usual way of life." (It took years before Daddy finally joined a church, thanks to my mother.)

"I remember batting flies to my brother at home once. He was catching them, throwing them back to me. A little pup about three months old was playing with us, running back and forth between us. So I threw the ball up in the air, ready to bat a fly out to my brother and WHACK! I hit the dog right in the head and killed him dead. I went over to Richard Farnum's and borrowed a spade from his grandfolks to bury the dog. It was one of the saddest days of my life."

"Mr. Layman, our principal, was really a nice fellow. One time, I was walking with one of the boys, and I met Mr. Layman on the street right in front of Billy Mathis' house. It was during baseball season and I happened to be smoking a cigarette. When I saw Mr. Layman, it was too late to throw it away, so I just turned the cigarette into the palm of my hand and put it in the pocket of my pants. Then I pushed the burning cigarette into the palm of my hand while I talked to Mr. Layman."

"During my junior and senior year, I worked down at Elmer's

Café on Main Street after school. On Saturdays and Saturday nights, I waited on customers, plus being the short order cook, and washed dishes. I remember I had a special egg sandwich I used to make. I'd stir it up real good, the whole thing, white and yellow all together, and then I'd deep fat fry it. Boy, it was delicious, this great big round egg. I worked all I could for fifty cents an hour. Sometimes I worked on Sundays, too. Once I worked eighty-four hours in a row, earning money for college. By the way, my dad told me that I didn't have the guts to go to college. He said I didn't have the guts to work for it!"

"The guys I ran around with liked to go to dances. A little town, called Linden, was just three or four miles from Prophetstown. We used to go over to dance, but they drank an awful lot which I didn't much care for. One time I took this girl over there, and when we came back to the car, I stepped on something – a great big round thing. It was real dark by the cars, but it felt like somebody's head! I got a match and looked down at it, and it WAS somebody's head. The guy had just passed clear out, right there by the car. We had to move him, so we could get out of the dance lot and go home. Most of the time, we went dancing on Saturday night at the Coliseum in Sterling. We'd go in Bob Brooks' car. Ben Pole would go with us, and Marvin Hunt and myself, and the girls. We'd go up on the second floor and dance to Wayne King and Guy Lombardo, or Sammy Kaye, Ben Bernie, Bart Castle, Clyde McCoy. One time, Deacon Jones was there. He sang a song that goes way back in history, 'If you can't give me beer, or big dollars, dear Lord, then give me those little sister quarters, dimes and nickels.''

"My Aunt Cora, my father's sister, came out from Boston again about this time. She's the one who helped me when I was out on the farm in Kansas and got my teeth fixed. This time she came to the house in Prophetstown. She kind of liked me, and she took an interest in what I was doing. This time, she fixed up my room. She took rags, old undershirts, sheets and things and tied them all together, and then dyed them purple. (Sounds like tie-dye, doesn't it?) She made me rag rugs, and she stained the floor in my bedroom, and made me curtains, all purple. I wound up having a beautiful room; I was really proud of it. We picked all the pears in the orchard, wrapped them up in newspaper and put them in a bag, so they wouldn't stain the nice new floor. Then she went back to Boston. All the pears rotted. I didn't know what to do with them. Nobody in my family liked pears. So, I finally threw them out."

"One of the highlights of my life in Prophetstown was the night that Bob Brooks, the 'aristocrat' at my high school, invited me to stay at his house. He drove a thirty-five Terraplane Essex with twelve cylinders. Man, that was the fastest car you ever saw in your life! It was quite an honor to stay at his house because he was the best boy in high school. His father had died, and his mother was left all the money from the farms. She gave Bob everything – clothes, cars. They lived on a farm. He had his own separate bath, all by himself. He took a bath before dinner, casually taking off his clothes and dropping them on the floor. When he came out, I went in. He had bath oil that you rub all over yourself – bath powder, too. Boy, this was really living! Bob was really a character. Sadly, he disappeared fighting on one of the islands in the Pacific during WW II, and they never found him."

"My senior play was probably (laughs) one of the most outstanding things in my high school career. It was sort of a villain thing. I was the 'mysterious Mr. King' which was the lead, but you know, I was pretty cocky in high school. I didn't learn my part, I didn't come to rehearsals on time and I about drove Miss Allen crazy. NOTE: As a drama director, I used to "love" these guys. "I got right up to the night of dress rehearsal, and realized, 'Gee, I don't know my lines! Then I went crazy, trying to learn my lines all that night and all the next day. When it came to the night of the play, and we got to the end where I'd stolen all the pearls, here came the owner of the pearls, the very wealthy owner of the house. I was looking in the dining room with the maid, my friend, Pud. I was supposedly having a love affair with her character, and the lady of the house came in to look for the pearls just as I found them. So, I dropped them right down the front of the maid's dress. There was a hook on the inside of her dress that the pearls were supposed to catch on, but they fell right through to the floor. I turned to the audience and said, 'Women don't wear enough clothes anymore,' and it brought down the house."

The summer after his senior year, Al Bell, Lloyd Junior, and his friends were given the opportunity to shock oats for a dollar a day. They shocked and shocked all morning, and then they were told they'd get a free dinner. "Well," Daddy told me, "the farmer had homebrew down in the well which made it real cool. So, we sat down on the porch, drank a bottle, ate dinner, had another bottle, and then the farmer told us it was time to go back to the field. Everyone returned to work when someone noticed Lloyd was missing. They asked me where he was, and I laughed. 'The homebrew put him to sleep. He's sound asleep on the farmer's porch for the rest of the afternoon.'"

Another time, the boys shocked rye. Daddy described it this way, "All the little sheaves are pointed. One can go in your sock and come right out the collar of your neck, it's so sticky. When I got home, I spent the rest of the night, picking rye grain from my clothes."

Daddy remembered his graduation night from high school, specifically for one dramatic moment. "My father came, and of course, my best girl friend. Everyone got their honors and diplomas, and when it was over, we marched backstage to the English room to take off our caps and gowns. Miss Block, the English and commercial teacher, isolated me, and said, 'Allen Bell, I want to say something even if you don't care.'"

Surprised, I said, 'Well, what did you want to say?'"

"She answered, 'With all of your talents, I just want you to do one thing. GET OUT OF THIS TOWN, AND DON'T YOU EVER COME BACK!'"

"Well, I'd worked at Elmer's all summer, and with my dad's dare that I 'didn't have the guts to go to college' ringing in my ear, I packed up my cousin Glen's old coat, plus those long pants with the pleats and huge cuffs that Aunt Cora had bought for me. Glen gave me a pair of golf knickers, the baggy kind that button below the knee, and with forty dollars in my pocket, I headed off to Illinois Wesleyan University."

## Chapter Thirteen

"When I got to Bloomington, the fraternities were rushing all the freshmen, me included. Hardly anybody had any money in those days, and I, in particular, had none except for my forty dollars. But a bunch of fellows and I finally decided on the Phi Gams. We went to live in their house to be rushed and pledged later on. My assigned roommate was Clayton Sturgeon. I wasn't especially crazy about Clayton, but he and I washed dishes for our meals. We didn't care about where we slept, as long as we had a place to sleep and got to go to school because that was a privilege in those days. Thanks to the Phi Gams, I didn't have to spend any of my forty dollars for food. It was 1933 – the worst year of the Great Depression."

"I met the Song Fellows when they sang at IWU. Harris White – he's still in Des Moines – was the second tenor. Stew Steelman was the first tenor. Wilbur Hatch was the original bass for the Song Fellows, and I can't remember the other fellow."

"I found out that as a liberal arts major, I could steal across the street and get one of those practice rooms in Presser Hall, so I could practice my homemade piano playing. And, I kept writing my father for more money. I suppose all college kids do. You know how it goes: The son writes his dad from college. 'No mun, no fun, your son.' The father writes back, 'Too bad, so sad, your dad.' My dad never did write to me, but he did send five dollars that first semester."

"Well, I finally had to pack up at the Phi Gam house because they finally realized what I'd known all along. I didn't have any money, and I wouldn't have any money. I went out looking for another room with Paul Wilson and a guy named Auggie. The three of us found another place – the Boy Scout Headquarters – fifth floor, down on

Main Street. We got our bunk beds in exchange for cleaning up there every Saturday morning. On school nights, I'd get to bed about two thirty in the morning; I was not an early morning riser. At six-thirty, Auggie and Paul would grab me by the shoulders and stand me on the floor. Those six-footers would get me between them, under each arm, give me some coffee, and then get me to school."

"My forty dollars lasted me until the end of October. I'd get a cup of coffee with all the refills I wanted, and a roll for five cents. That's all I'd have. I was busy at school, anyhow. At night, I'd get coffee or milk for five cents, and a nickel for a hamburger for my supper. That was twenty cents a day…until Web Wykoff's." (Story on Web just ahead.)

That first year, Al Bell hitchhiked home to try to get money from his dad. He didn't get any, but his dad did take him out for dinner. On the way back to college, he got a ride from a guy in a pickup who was wearing brand new overalls and a new straw hat. "I kept pumping him, talking about being a farmer, his crops and everything, when all of a sudden, he pulled a pistol from between the seats! 'What's th-th-that for?' I asked.

'Just in case I get stopped by the Feds," he answered.

'Why?' I asked.

'The back of this truck is solid,' he said. 'Instead of a stock rack, it's a square barrel. It holds one hundred fifty gallons of pure alcohol.'

'Is there any in there now?'

'You betcha,' he said, 'and if we get stopped, you better start running!'"

"I remember getting terrible grades the first semester – in fact, the whole first year. I never had any time to study. I was too busy trying to make money to stay in school and feed myself. I'd work nights until two in the morning, and then run over to the Boy Scout Headquarters, run up five flights of stairs, and my roommates would be sleeping away. At six, they'd roll me out of bed and run me to school. I took German the first year and got a D minus! English was a C, so was American History. 'Reflective Thinking'. That was a snap course with Professor Brown. He was an authority on President Lincoln, if I remember rightly. He was a very humorous man because he never knew, really, what was going on. He was just sort of an oddball, so I slept through most of his ten to eleven o'clock class. I mean, you can't work all night and be awake from ten to eleven the next morning! But he'd always give the roll call. I sat down front with the A's and B's, and he'd say, 'Master Alsop? Amunds, Bell?' We'd all say 'Present', and then he'd say, 'Miss Benson, Master Bates?', and everybody would roar hysterically."

"My German teacher was Professor Ferguson." Daddy's eyes softened. "I have an eight by ten picture of him as he looked over his glasses…wonderful old man. I think he lived to be about eighty years old. The dean of the liberal arts school, Dean Wallace, taught American History. He was really great. He lived it out. He'd get up on the desk with his yardstick and row across the Potomac. Because I didn't do so well in German, I had to take it all over again the next summer. I got a B in a six week course at Illinois State Normal (which was near Wesleyan). The instructor was sort of a mannish woman, but a really wonderful teacher. She liked me, and I was inspired by her. That's when I got a hold of this studying business, and I really began to study."

Daddy said that he'd go down to the pool hall in Bloomington off and on. "One night, there was a big shot politician by the name of Jake Ward. Well, I was cussing and swearing and carrying on, and he stopped me. 'You know something, Al Bell?'

"I said, 'Huh?'"

'Do you know why people swear?' he asked."

'Whaddya mean, why do people swear?' I said. 'It sorta expresses yourself.'"

"He explained. 'As a matter of fact, the reason people swear is because they don't know the right word to put in the proper spot. Instead of saying, 'He's an imbecilic character', they say, 'the blankety blank-blank doesn't know a blankety blank about anything.'

"He concluded, 'Only stupid people swear.' And you know something? I quit swearing that night.'"

Daddy didn't remember exactly how he got moved into Grandma Lampke's down on Front Street. "I think that Clayton Sturgeon and I answered the same ad in the newspaper. And this about leads me up to Web Wykoff and the Front Street Café. I'd been going for weeks on my twenty cent a day diet. Every day after school, I'd look for ANY kind of job available, because, man, you get hungry on twenty cents a day, and I was just about to run out of money. I only had a couple dollars left."

"I heard about a new café opening up on Front Street, so I walked into this place. You could tell it was brand new. There was a small, thin, neatly dressed, gray-haired man. He looked me up and down when I asked for a job and said, 'Everyone we need has just been hired yesterday. It you'd been here yesterday, I'd had a job for ya. Sorry.' I started to go, and he asked me, 'Buddy…When'd you eat last?'"

"I turned back to him. 'That, Sir, is none of your business.'"

"He said, 'I'm sorry. Hey Joe! Bring us over a couple of chicken dinners. You'll stay and talk to me, won't ya?'"

"'Not if it's for charity,' I said."

'It's not,' he replied. 'Maybe I can think of something that will do you some good.' So we sat down at a table, and after a while, Web asked, 'Tell me. Do you have a white shirt and blue or black pants?' I had the shirt. I wasn't worried about the trousers. I'd worry about that later."

"'Okay,' he said. 'You get 'em and be here at eight o'clock tonight.' I thought that I'd be out front as a waiter, but when I came back, he put me back in the kitchen, washing dishes."

"About eight-thirty that night, I was going like mad, getting a little dishwater on my pants and shirt, when who should walk into the restaurant but Clayton Sturgeon. He came back to the kitchen with a policeman who said, 'Is this the guy?'"

'Yeah, he's the one,' Clayton said.

'Do you want to prefer charges?' the policeman asked.

'Nah,' he said. "Just the pants is all I want.' So I took the pants off and stood there with my short and shirts on, and after I'd washed dishes for about an hour and a half, I said to the cook, 'Hey, do you have any pants I could wear?' He was a little guy, about five foot two or three."

'Well, you can have my extra pair of cook pants,' he said. I put them on, and they were short. Very, very short. They came just below my knees. See, what had happened was that when I'd gotten back to the room to dress for my new job, I had the white shirt, just like I said, but I didn't have any blue or black trousers. Clayton did, so I figured I'd just ask him for them. However, Clayton didn't come home and didn't come home, and it was about seven o'clock, so I just took the trousers. I figured I'd tell him about it when he got home. Anyway, after working until midnight that night, I went home wearing the cook's white trousers."

"Later on that week, I worked out front with trousers that I'd borrowed from another guy. The first or second night out front, I got fifteen dollars tip from waiting on people who'd been drinking too much. The next day, I went out and bought my first pair of teal blue trousers."

"I remember one night when I was working at Web's, and the cook said to me, 'Hey, did you ever steal a knife?' Well, I appreciated what he'd done for me, and I didn't understand what he meant by 'steeling a knife', which means using a big steel to sharpen a knife."

"I said, 'No sir. I never stole a knife, but you tell me what kind of knife you want, and I'll go steal it!'"

"Web Wykoff lived dangerously in those days. After all he'd done for me, saving me when I was down to my last buck, I was with him all the way. This was back in Prohibition time, remember. I learned that Web paid off city officials. He paid off policemen, so he could bring alcohol by the barrel and truck it from Chicago. The policeman on the beat was the key guy, so by paying him off, the cop would time his rounds, so he'd be there at the wrong time when the alcohol came in."

"One night about one a.m., the truck from Chicago came in with a barrel of alcohol. I helped roll it into the restaurant after we got it off the truck. We rolled it downstairs where we'd pull up the floor back of the bar, and after we'd taken the empty barrel out, we'd put the new one in. We'd cover it all up again and hook the pipes up to the pop dispenser, and then cover up the hole. We'd just gotten the barrel in the door that night when a strange policeman came around the door – one o'clock at night – and the liquor truck was still parked out front. We got the barrel to the head of the stairs, and I yelled to Web, 'Hey! There's a cop out front! What'll we do?'"

'Stall him!' he answered, 'while we bury the barrel.'

"I wanted to say 'How?' but the barrel was halfway down the stairs, and the cop was coming in the front door. So, I grabbed a big tray of dirty dishes and backed down the stairs. Then I started up the stairs again. Here I was, coming up the stairs with a great big tray full of dirty dishes and glasses, purposely running into a policeman."

'Let me past ya!' the cop demanded.

'I can't!' I said. 'I'm sorry sir, but I've got to get upstairs with these dishes.'

"The cop retorted, 'Well, I've got to get DOWNstairs and see what's going on.'"

'Yes, sir, just a minute,' I stalled. 'If you'll just back up the stairs, I'll come up with the tray and get out of your way.'

'Now, you let me...' the policeman pushed.

"'No sir,' I insisted. 'I've got to get up there with these dirty dishes. The boss'll fire me if I drop these dirty dishes!'"

"'Oh, all right.' He gave in, backing clear up to the top of the stairs."

"I took my time, of course, and finally reached the top of the stairs. By that time, the barrel was hidden in the basement floor, and everyone was sitting around, drinking pop or coffee."

Daddy continued, "Many times, we had mayors and senators, congressmen and other city officials down there in Web Wykoff's basement, and they tipped well. After a couple weeks or so, I bought an eighteen dollar suit, and I bought a forty dollar, grey sharkskin business suit for a dollar a week – forty weeks. It was tailor-fitted, and I wore it for years and years. I began to hate it – I'd worn it so long. Finally, after I met my wife, I remember I bought a black and white checked 'gambler's suit', probably under the influence of Web Wykoff. It was tailor-made and cost me all of twenty-two dollars and fifty cents. My wife still has a piece of it someplace at home."

"As time went on, Grandma Lampke and I got friendlier. I was always nice to older ladies anyway. I found out that if I could get another roomer or two, I could get my rent free. All I'd have to do is make the beds and clean up the place and help her on Saturdays. Because Grandma was pretty hard up, I went out to find a couple more boys for the place. I got Elmer Hastings after Clayton moved out. Elmer was half mad; I didn't care. Elmer was later killed in a test dive over Texas after he'd enlisted in World War II. Then Chuck Acre moved in, and I found 'Stretch' Miller for Elmer, and I lived with Chuck. Stretch Miller was about six foot four. He went with one of the most beautiful girls on campus, Elizabeth Ann Goudy. She was nearly six foot two, herself. Anyway, Stretch became a sports announcer. I never liked him very much because he drooled on his pillow when he slept, and I'd have to make the beds the next morning."

"Grandpa Lampke's house wasn't exactly modern; they had an outhouse out back. Chuck Acre was from Chicago, and he wasn't too crazy about it, so he invented a little 'dealie' up in our closet. He drilled a little hole, stuck a pipe through it to the outside, and stuck a funnel into the pipe. That was our bathroom for the winter! How Grandma found out about it, I don't know but when she discovered it, she just raised heck and screamed until the cows came home. And of course, she made Chuck take it out. In those days, Chuck Acre was stringing tennis rackets for an income, besides going to school. He'd get about five dollars a racket. Last I knew he was in advertising in Chicago."

"It was a good place to live. Grandma had a piano, so I learned how to play better. It used to bother Grandpa, but then he became hard of hearing, and it didn't bother him as much. I still smoked; Grandpa had pipe tobacco, and we'd sit and smoke and listen to their radio: Fred Allen, Eddie Cantor, Parky Carcass, Joe 'I hope, I hope, I hope' Penner, and City Service Hour, the Lone Ranger, and Amos and Andy at ten o'clock every night."

"That fall, Grandpa Lampke had a stroke while sitting in his chair. Grandma and I carried him to bed. When he'd recovered enough, I'd help him get up around seven every morning, get him washed and dressed, and shave his whiskers. Grandma gave me toast and coffee – that's how she started giving me my meals. Grandpa couldn't talk much after the stroke. He'd just sit in his old leather chair and grunt whenever you talked to him. He always seemed to be mad. I don't suppose he was; he was just miserable. Sunday nights, we'd listen to the radio, and I'd laugh. If it got pretty hysterical, Grandma would laugh, and Grandpa would just sit there and smile a little bit. After Grandpa died, Grandma took part of the insurance money and built a sort of bathroom part way up the stairs. It curved to the left and back again, so you had to sneak through the bathroom to get upstairs!"

"The second year at college was a little bit better. I got much better grades in German. I sat right next to Paul Lambert who later became an eye specialist in Des Moines. I had to battle Paul for grades because he'd come from a German community in Milwaukee. His family spoke German all the time at home. I finally bested him by one point. After school, I'd play ping pong at the Italian variety store. I got pretty good at ping pong, too."

"Chapel at school was real interesting, except on Wednesdays when a minister would come and speak. Sometimes the Song Fellows would sing. Jodie Marshall, I think that was her name, would sit on the piano and sing like Helen Morgan. I tried out for the chorus and made it. I sang bass in 'The Messiah'; I just loved Handel's music. Dean

Westbrook was the conductor." NOTE: My sister Rhea reminded me that our mother was Dean Westbrook's secretary. They communicated for years. And when Rhea attended Drake University, Dean Westbrook was one of her teachers!

"Bill Austin, who was the pianist for the Song Fellows, was a good friend of mine. We used to eat at the Post Office Café which was right across the street from the Post Office, of course. Talk about prices! You'd get lunch for twenty cents, and if you wanted pie, you got it for a nickel. The restaurant did so well that people had to stand in line, just like they would stand in line for stamps. We had to eat really fast because people were waiting in line behind you. Well, they did so well that the guy bought the Majestic Café up the street which held two or three hundred customers, but the big crowd didn't look so big in there. He went broke because people thought the café was empty all the time!"

Al Bell and Chuck Acre were friends for a long time. I remember hearing many stories about the two of them when I was growing up. Daddy continued, "Chuck had been at Valpo (Valparaiso University outside of Chicago) before he came to Wesleyan, and it was at Valpo that he met Hoagy Carmichael. Hoagy was still playing dance bands back then." (Hoagy Carmichael is best known for writing and playing the hit pop ballad, 'Stardust'. Watch the classic film, 'The Best Years of Our Lives'" to see Hoagy in action!) "I found out later that Chuck had been trying to get me moved into Grandma Lampke's house, so HE could get part of his room rent deducted!"

"As I recall, I paid two dollars a week for my room rent, and I'd gotten about thirty dollars behind. I was hired at Schleswig Lumber and Coal Company to shovel coal in a one hundred fifteen ton hopper car. It took me almost all the next summer to catch up on rent."

"Then there was the time that Chuck and I promoted the Junior and Senior dance at the Shrine Auditorium in Bloomington. He supplied the band; in truth, he engineered most of it. We got a hold of 'Floyd Towne and His Band of Renown.' Old timers can remember that Dusty Rhodes was his singer. Dusty went on to have his own orchestra. We charged all the kids a dollar a piece, and Chuck made five hundred dollars net. In those days, that was a fortune! He gave me fifty dollars for helping him put up bills (flyers) and for keeping my mouth shut regarding how much he'd made!"

"Then I went on to take my great histrionical (sic) talents to the radio station in town, WJBC. At first, I played music and spot announcements, and then through my various sneaky sources, I started a gossip program called 'The Man About Town.' I'd tell about who was where when, who went to the Capital Theater, and I got free tickets, of course. Any time I mentioned a commercial place, they'd always say, 'Oh, here's a couple tickets to come to our show or dance. I remember the theme song I chose for that show was a Mills Brothers' hit. (Singing) "Oh, I heard. Yes, I heard. Oh, it wasn't told to me, I only heard'."

"The first time my future wife heard me on the radio was in Springfield in 1934. I was announcing for a walkathon, which she thought was terrible." ('They Shoot Horses, Don't They?' is an effective film showing a dance-a-thon from that era.) "Now, a walkathon contest was an endurance contest where couples joined up to see which couple could walk the farthest, with sprints every two or three hours to wear out the weaker entrants. After that, it was really sort of horrible. It went on until just one couple was left standing. It went something like this, 'Ladies and gentlemen! We are now down to only three couples, and there's old Joe and Sadie – they're going down, they're going down.' The orchestra would be playing a drum roll. 'She's down on the floor. Watch him now. He's trying to pull her back up again. He's almost asleep himself. Ladies and gentlemen, this is the most exciting thing you've ever seen...' And that's the way we would describe the action at a walkathon."

Al Bell's face lit up. "One day, I overheard the sales manager at the radio station tell the manager, Mr. McGregor, that they were going to lose the Schleswig Lumber and Coal account, unless they came up with something really good. Well, I got together with Chuck Acre, and we created, 'Jasper and Jeremiah', a name for a black face skit. I'd shoveled coal for the company so I knew who the boss was, and I went to him with this idea. Then Chuck and I went down to the radio station and sold them on the idea. We had that account for a couple years. Incidentally, I don't think Mr. Schleswig ever figured out that I was the same guy who'd shoveled coal for him to pay for my rent the first year!"

"All the time I was living with Chuck at Mrs. Lampke's, he was going with a girl named Jackie Hoover. She was from Chicago, too. They decided to get married, so Chuck took me to Chicago with him to be his best man. We got Jackie's brother's car and drove into Chicago.

You talk about a scary ride! On the south side of Chicago, when we stopped for a railroad crossing and a red light, a man tried to get into the car. He just fought and fought and fought. After the wedding on our way back to Bloomington, I was driving Jackie's car. Around Cicero, a really wicked town, I ran right over, or rather straddled, a headless and legless corpse some gangster had just thrown out."

"I believe it was the next summer that I got a job as a lifeguard out at Lake Bloomington." Daddy paused. "How I ever did all these things with holes in my heart, I'll never know. Anyway, I was the lifeguard and sat up on the tall chair, waiting for people to drown. Web Wykoff got the concessions at the lake and served chicken dinners. I helped him out there, as well. I also worked at a restaurant owned by a guy named Paul who had a silver plate in his head from an auto accident. I had to drive for him because every so often that plate would press on his brain, and he was apt to drive off into the ditch."

"That fall, Web Wykoff started a gambling den on a side street in town. It was hard to find, but you'd go up these stairs, and there would be a dark door with a kind of mirror on it and a peephole. You'd knock on the door, and a deep voice would say, 'Who sent ya?' You'd knock three times again, and say, 'Web sent me.' There was a buzzer, and you'd push the door open while the buzzer was buzzing. I also worked at the Green Mill Café. They were Greek – really great people. I washed dishes, bussed tables, anything they needed me to do. Guys were always coming in from Chicago or St. Louis, asking for jobs. I remember George, the cook. He'd always talk about his hopes and what he wanted to do."

"Just around the corner from the Green Mill was the Front Street Theatre. I used to walk by there every day. I finally got up my nerve and asked the manager for a job. I think his name was Monty Montgomery. He surprised me when he said, 'How'd ya like to usher for me and see the shows for free?' See the shows free, and they would pay ME? After six months, he made me Assistant Manager. I sold tickets, took the money and he was gone. He trusted me. On Saturdays, I worked until eleven o'clock at the Green Mill, and then I'd run like mad to the theatre and sell tickets until five o'clock. Then I'd run back to the Green Mill and work the supper hour until about six forty-five, and then run like the dickens back to the theatre and work until about ten thirty. After I got all my tickets to match, I'd run back to the Green Mill until the late crowd left, about four or five in the morning. I'd walk about a mile and a half home and get to bed around five-thirty in the morning. No wonder I never got to church in those days. Two holes in my heart, plus several in my head… plus a few rocks."

"I almost forgot about the amateur talent contest at Normal. (The two towns are right next to each other.) It was held at some church, and they were trying out for WLS (Chicago) characters, like Lulu Belle Scott, the Arkansas Woodchopper, the Mazurek Sisters, and Uncle Ezra. I tried out for Uncle Ezra, and because I could impersonate him, I won the part. Then I asked what they paid to do the part, and they said, 'Oh, my goodness sake. You're going to stand up here in front of all your neighbors and friends, and they'll see you doing the famous Uncle Ezra character from Chicago."

I looked at them and said, 'You take the glory. I'll take the cash.' That was it. I was out of the contest."

Al Bell and Rhea Morgan about the time
they met at Illinois Wesleyan University

Becky Bell-Greenstreet | 97

# Chapter Fourteen

"Then on October 12, 1935, I met Rhea Morgan, a Delta Omicron (music sorority) from Springfield, Illinois. Chuck Acre came home from school and told me he was producing a college play on WJBC. He said, 'I've really got a great gal for you this time! She's in this play, so I'll introduce you two tonight.'"

"Ooooh...Not another blonde!"

'No,' he said. 'She's little, she's curly haired and she has big brown sparkly eyes. You'll love her!'"

"Oh no," I groaned.

'Ah, come on, Al, please. You'll like her,' Chuck urged.

"It went on like that, until finally, I went to the radio station. I sat down at the piano and started singing and playing some of the popular tunes I'd figured out, and here came some students, trouping through the studio. I looked them over. Then Chuck appeared with the last two girls. There she was – everything Chuck had promised – plus a little shy. Chuck introduced us. I was just playing some arpeggio chords, and asked her, 'What would you like me to play?' She batted those sparkly brown eyes. Little did I know how terribly nervous she was."

NOTE: Mother's version revealed her paralyzed state at meeting Al Bell. She had heard of him, the Don Juan of the campus. She knew from her friends that girls were crazy over him, and that he could get any girl he wanted. Besides, she was shy and figured she was much too inexperienced for someone like him. She tried desperately to think of a song to request. Nothing. Absolutely no song came to her mind, except for one which she refused to say because of the lyrics.

Al Bell asked her again. "What would you like me to play?" Finally, her mouth opened. All she could say was, 'You Made Me Love You.' He began singing and playing to her, and that moment became family history.

# Chapter Fifteen

## "SONS OF OKEFENOKEE"

Rivulets of perspiration streamed like salty summer rain down my flushed face. My eyes burned from the relentless noonday sun. Inside my tight-fitting, overly starched dress, this bulging, budding, wanna-be actress suffered silently, and listened obediently to my father's directions:

1. Pole the boat to my right for a SLOW count of ten.
2. Look over my shoulder toward the camera and appear to see nothing.
3. Do a doubletake, realizing there really was an alligator following the boat.
4. Frantically resume poling the boat.
5. Pitch myself backwards OUT of the boat and into the water.

Daddy had promised that this wasn't dangerous. The fact that he had sent my mother to town on a made-up errand wasn't a tip-off to me, the gullible ten year old, in the least. "After all," he assured me, "there will be four men in the water out of camera range who will be poking long poles in the water to keep alligators away from the boat." (I was a good swimmer, so what's the problem?) "Better not swim back to the boat too well," he added. "We want the kids to think you don't know how to swim, so they'll get more excited. Just dog paddle, and make it look sloppy. Lots of splashing, okay?"

It was June of 1957. I was the star of this movie which would be shown to almost every small school in Iowa that September. I really had no idea how this scene, the climax of the movie, would affect audiences until Al Bell came to my own school. Daddy always touted the maxim that "A prophet is without honor in his own hometown." However, the moment "Susie" fell out of the boat, quickly followed by close-ups of alligators in hot pursuit, the darkened gymnasium packed with 300 kids from five to eighteen, became a deafening inferno of spontaneous screams. After the show, my peers demanded, "How could you DO that?" All I could honestly say was, "Daddy told me to." (No wonder I got no respect from the high schoolers.)

Every other summer, my folks would take a trip within the continental United States and Canada, so that Mother wouldn't have to be away from us kids. Daddy preferred the trips with just Mother, but these trips were cheaper, and his wife was pacified. When the entire family traveled together, we camped out in a tent, cooking over a Coleman gas stove, but after my older siblings had gone off to college, the four of us slept in the car (the trademark red and white station wagon seen in many of the earlier movies.) First, we folded down the back seat. Then we lugged my folks' mattress out of the house, and pushing and pulling, filled up the back of the car with it. My little brother was only six, so for his bed, Daddy rigged up a sheet of plywood, stretching it across the back of the car between the windows and above the big mattress. I slept in the front seat. Inevitably, every night on the road, a loud noise (bears?), would cause me to rise up, banging my head on the steering wheel. It never occurred to me to simply turn around with my feet beneath the wheel.

One sweltering afternoon, en route to Georgia, Mother rode in the back of the car with my brother and me. Her purpose was to dye my hair light blonde. "But it'll look awful when it grows out," I whined. (And, sure enough, a tenth grade girl behind me in the bleachers at the Al Bell show that fall, whispered loudly to a friend how despicable my hair looked.) As usual, Daddy had the final word, "Blonde hair shows up better in the movies." Sitting on that mattress in the back of the car for two days, Doug and I were already stoop-shouldered from trying to look out the windows. Now, we had to inhale ammonia for a couple hours, while Rhea Bell transformed her ash blonde ugly duckling into a flaxen-haired "star."

In order to save money (which was my father's guiding principle throughout his life), we always ate lunch in the car. Daddy drove; Mother would make sandwiches, usually bologna (baloney) for us kids and a peanut butter and jelly for desert. Lettuce, tomato, and mayonnaise were always in the cooler at Mother's feet, and Daddy's braunschweiger or liverwurst required a thick piece of onion. Daily aromas in the car included overripe bananas, loose grapes that rolled under the seats, and homemade chocolate chip and peanut butter cookies, dozens of them, packed into every little cranny of the car. By the end of the third day on the road, my brother and I were five pounds heavier and matted with crumbs.

This trip, Daddy had decided to invest in a (cheap) motel room during our stay, which was, unquestionably, a lifesaver since summer in southern Georgia is a total meltdown. On the days when our parents were shooting either scenery or Al Bell's scenes as the park guide, Doug and I spent many oppressive afternoons cooling off in the garbage-strewn river behind the motel. NOTE: Few kids recognized Al Bell as the guide in this movie because, for the first and last time in any of his movies, he was clean shaven. Of course, any Al Bell aficionado would have picked up on the bright red shirt he wore. ("It shows up better in the movie.")

Our watering hole, though cooler than being outside, was chock full of rusty tin cans, sharp rocks, floating debris, and several other desperate, sweaty kids. Hanging out in that toxic river was still preferable to dying from the muggy, buggy steam in our motel room. For some reason, probably our northern accents, bullies tended to pick on my brother and me, so after we'd had enough, we'd head back to the room and play card games like Crazy Eights, Rummy, or Doug's favorite, War. He insisted that we sit in the dark because it felt cooler. The motel owner's son, who was about my age, occasionally invited us down to their air-conditioned apartment for a pineapple sandwich (canned pineapple slices, bread and butter for those who care). He was very curious about our dad's business, so we really stretched out the story as we cooled off.

On the days Doug and I were needed at the swamp, I always had to wear my costume. Mother had made me a frilly pink dress (Aha! Is that why I don't like pink?), complete with scratchy lace and layers of petticoats. My hair in those days was extraordinarily thick. Mother pulled it back into a long, tight ponytail, so tight that it felt like not only were my eyebrows raised, but I felt like I had a perpetual grin.
We would shoot as many scenes as possible in the relatively cooler morning, and then retire to the concession area to regroup and refresh ourselves for a while. The dimly lit cabin (one of the few enclosed buildings at the time) sold concessions and souvenirs. (I brought

home a green, scaly, alligator ashtray. It was all I could afford.) Our table sat right under a ceiling fan that just barely stirred the air. Doug and I would sit, and, oh, so slowly, sip our icy RC colas, dreading the moment that Daddy would announce that it was time to go back to work. Doug's cameo in the movie was that of a tourist, watching a monkey in a cage. Daddy told me that we had to establish Susie's character as an obnoxious kid by stealing a banana stashed in Doug's back pocket, just before I ran off to steal a rowboat. The irony was, of course, that I was the most innocent person in the family. How many times in my childhood did I hear, "We're not being mean; it's just so easy to tease you!"

One particularly miserable afternoon, we had been filming a trained baby black bear that was chained to a post inside a tent. (My sensitivities for animal rights are much more heightened these days.) We were told the bear loved RC cola, so naturally Susie was told to feed the bear an RC for the camera. When on his hind legs, this "baby" stood as tall as I. His long claws groped desperately for the bottle of pop in my hand, while Daddy yelled instructions from behind the camera. "GET CLOSER TO HIM!" (Closer? His hot breath felt like steam on my trembling hand.)

"But he'll bite me!" I whined from one side of my mouth.

"Walk! Move! Get him into the light and STAY THERE!" he directed. I'd dive in close, the RC would gush out of the bottle and up the bear's nose. He'd lunge, I'd duck. We were both covered with sticky, foamy syrup by the time Daddy yelled, "STOP!" and then he grumbled, "I don't know if that's going to come out or not" shaking his head disparagingly at his cowardly daughter.

We all agreed that it was time we were treated to an RC, so we headed for our refuge and ordered our usual. After a few swallows of his, Daddy began to blow into the bottle, making fairly musical sounds. I joined in, and although it took several tries for little Doug and my lady-like mother to learn how to shape their lips just right, we soon had a quartette of pitches, "Oompah-pahing" like a calliope. "Let's tune up. Mother, you and I will be in octaves. Now, Doug you take a drink, just a little one." Our major chord had become a minor seventh! "Doug, take a medium sized sip. We're going to make a major seventh chord!" Of course, we'd garnered the attention of everyone in the canteen, but all that Doug and I cared about was being out of the heat for as long as possible. Daddy was just having his regular good time, entertaining the other guests in the room.

One morning, the manager of the swamp located us as we were filming Susie watch otters at play. "Get over to the barn, quick! They've brought in some sacks of live rattlers!" We trailed our father who loved getting serendipitous footage on the spur of the moment. It was a good scene, filming the snake handlers who were transferring snakes from burlap sacks to wooden boxes. Then Al Bell got an inspiration.

"We've got to have a scene where a snake drops into Susie's boat!" I never questioned my father's plans. I whined a lot, but I knew better than to argue with the boss. Daddy borrowed a nonpoisonous, but nonetheless, big and scary-looking snake from one of the park exhibits. I'm really lucky that snakes didn't spook me like spiders did. Even Daddy couldn't have made me get in the same scene with the wolf spider that he shot for a scene later in the movie. (If you don't know, wolf spiders are the size of your hand, or bigger.) Every time I saw that scene in the movie, I shut my eyes.

This snake was easily four feet long. We set up the scene so that it appeared that I was resting in the boat, sadly surveying my situation at being hopelessly lost in the swamp. The boat was actually moored to a tree on shore, so that the snake handler could lean in out of camera range and hang the snake in the tree. "Now, when the snake drops into the boat," Daddy instructed me, "you stand up and scream, okay?" Until that moment, I was to be totally oblivious to the fact that a snake was indeed going to drop in beside me. There are a couple times in the film where I anticipated what was about to happen, the sure sign of an amateur actor; however, when that fifteen pound reptile dropped, "Thud!" on my Mary Janes, I was genuinely terrified. Weeks later, as we sat on the dining room floor, dubbing in the sound, with the action rolling from the projector, I couldn't recreate the fear I'd felt, so it's my mother's high-pitched scream that made the movie, not mine.

Although Mother spent hours and hours planning the itinerary for the trip, researching countless books and setting up reservations, Al Bell often improvised his plots. I remember him thinking out loud in the car on the way down, "Let's see. We'll have this spoiled little rich girl from Palm Springs, see. And Mother, you'll play her snooty mother, who leaves her for the day to see the swamp. Yeah, that's it." Quite often, Daddy filmed the plot as he composed it. Fortunately, he could film a lot of animals and scenery while he thought up the ending.

The park had many animals exhibited. When Daddy saw a descented skunk in an exhibit, he created a scene where Susie, who was lost, wandered across a small island. "When you see the skunk, pretend that it's a kitty cat. It'll be behind the log, so you'll be the only one to actually see it at first. Pick it up, nice and high, so the camera can see it; then pet it like crazy. Let's see a great big smile like you love kitties. Then, at the moment when you realize it's a skunk, look directly at the camera with an 'Uh-Oh' look. Very carefully, set the skunk back down, and run like heck out of camera range." For once, my timing was perfect, and this proved to be one of the funniest moments in the film.

What I admired most about Daddy's films was his skill in selecting appropriate music for the soundtrack. Depending on the country, of course, he would choose German polka music (Austria), or Spanish flamenco (Spain), and so on. Frequently, he paired up classical music with many scenes, including most of "Sons of Okefenokee." One of the most visually beautiful scenes in this movie was taken from the top of a ranger tower. (Daddy climbed many steps, slowly, to do this.) First, he set me up down below, poised to pole my boat through a narrow canal, bordered with cypress trees that literally dripped Spanish moss. He signaled Mother on the ground who motioned for me to start poling. This verdant bird's eye view is complemented with the lush, haunting sounds of Stravinsky's "Firebird Suite." (Mother turned Daddy on to classical music and by the time he was a filmmaker, he owned every "Best of..." album he could find, from Beethoven to Rimsky-Korsakov to the soundtrack of the film, "Around the World in 80 Days".)

Much of Okefenokee Swamp, especially the little islands, floats; that is, the soil is just a few inches deep, sitting on water. Daddy boldly stepped onto the first one, then directed me to follow. I was really skeptical, because I could see my dad teetering, arms stretched out for balance, as he took tentative steps. Of course, a scene had to be filmed here, so the Iowa kids could see Susie teetering, too, so I reluctantly left the safety of the boat. It was eerie, walking, or more precisely, sinking, into this floating scenery, but I gradually quit trembling and got used to it. The blend of music, scenery, and an authentic soundtrack of exotic birds calling, frogs croaking, and the almost, but not quite, audible gliding of alligators and other slithering creatures through the murky, green waters, lent a surreal quality to many of the swamp scenes.

Mother has said (and I remember) that she and my dad argued frequently about the artistic "framing" of many scenes, so Al Bell would often shoot the scene two ways just to please her. She admitted that when they got home, and he would show her the choices, she would invariably choose his shot. On the day Daddy shot the film's climax, that of me falling out of the boat, he made an executive decision. By sending my mother into town on an "important" errand, he could have total control of this crucial scene without consulting anyone. God knows that his "star" wasn't going to voice her objections. In fact, I was so focused on doing the scene right the first time, that I didn't even realize my mother was gone. There was such an air of importance about this scene, that I just kept my mouth shut and waited for directions. The manager of the park who watched that day's filming, had loaned Daddy some of his best men, actual alligator wrestlers, to keep watch on the water around my boat, in hopes that no 'gator would slip through this crucial ring of action. It never occurred to me that underneath the algae-ridden water, there were all kinds of creepy crawlers besides alligators!

Mother had earlier fixed my (bleached) golden ponytail just so, dressed me in my prissy pink dress, and trusted Daddy to wait until she got back to continue shooting. Now, I had spent several weeks learning how to follow my dad's directorial commands. He never hollered, "Action." As I recall, the most formal announcement he may have given was, "Get ready…The camera's rolling, GO!"

The first take was as smooth as if I'd had a stunt double; I spontaneously flipped out the back of the boat. My clumsy attempts to appear to be a non-swimmer resulted in so much splashing that I couldn't see where I was going, but Daddy loved it. I swam back up on shore where Mother had arrived. She was apoplectic and yelled condemnations at her foolish husband. Before she could get in too many protestations, however, he announced loudly, "We're going to have to do it again; I think I had the lens cap on." (Sometimes things happened too fast in this basically one-man show, and Daddy would get flustered, tossing his light meter over his back or fumbling with the tripod.)

"Get Becky dried off, fix her hair and dry her dress, and let's do another shot," he ordered. My mother dutifully led me off to the women's restroom, both of us grumbling all the way. Thank goodness, hand dryers had been invented by then. Fifteen minutes later, we came out ready to do the scene again. We managed to shoot the scene TWICE more that day, but the second and third times, I wasn't very spontaneous about falling out of the boat.

"The water goes up my nose!" I wailed. As it turned out, the best take was the first (good) one.

The final scene, where my snotty movie mother returns to find me a sopping mess, was a wide shot. Daddy had placed the camera and tripod twenty feet or so away, so that all three of us could be in the picture. Daddy's "Aw, shucks" tour guide stood behind me, expecting thanks for rescuing this irritating brat. Mother and I ran toward each other in a very real embrace. Her broad brimmed hat flew off, and Mother went down on her knees where I threw myself into her arms. Since my mom was rarely this effusive, I enjoyed the filming and viewing of this reunion scene.

That next winter, while Al Bell was showing that movie to thousands of kids all over Iowa, I, like many of those kids, came down with the Russian flu. After each show, he would ask "his kids" to wish Susie well. As I lay, feverish and nauseous on the couch, I read dozens of "Get Well" cards, most of them handmade with an entire class of signatures. It was my first exposure to being famous, and I rather liked it. I owe Al Bell for that…and much, much more.

Becky Bell just before the bleach job.

## Chapter Sixteen

### "SONS OF NEW YORK CITY"

$C$*LOSEUP OF YOUNG GIRL'S FINGER TRACING AN ENDLESS LIST OF "JOHN JOHNSONS" IN THE NEW YORK CITY PHONE BOOK. AS SHE TURNS PAGE AFTER PAGE, WE HEAR THE VOICEOVER IN HER PSEUDO SCANDINAVIAN ACCENT:* "Yon Yonson, Yon Yonson, Yon Yonson...Yumpin' Yiminee! Vich vun is Gronpah??"

At Mother's urging, Daddy reluctantly agreed to film within the continental United States for every other movie, so that the family could be together. This would be my second lead role, after "Susie" had successfully gained a following after being lost in the Okefenokee Swamp two years earlier.

Daddy's plot for the New York City movie was quite simple: I would portray "Greta" a newly arrived immigrant, searching for her grandfather who lived somewhere in New York City. It was no surprise that her search took her all over the city, so that Iowa schoolkids could experience not only famous landmarks and monuments, but the hustle and bustle of what was then the largest city in the world. It was June of 1959, and I was twelve years old.

Every morning, Mother would Frenchbraid my hair into two pigtails, complete with red ribbons, and I would don my immigrant costume. Anyone who has experienced NYC in the summer knows how very hot and humid the city can be. Loose, light, abbreviated clothing would have been tolerable in June, but I perspired through the streets and sights of New York in not only a long, dark skirt, but a sweater and knee high socks. (Naturally, the sweater was Al Bell Red, "You have to show up in every scene!") Passersby in sleeveless shirts and shorts gawked at this chubby, ugly duckling, sweating in winter garb. After a couple weeks, I finally got used to it…the costume, not the staring.

We followed several trip traditions. Before leaving our farm outside Menlo, I continued my habit of writing myself a "welcome home" note and taping it to my bedroom door. This helped to alleviate my fears, I think, that the big, bad city might change me in some way. New York held mystery, glamour, romance. Perhaps I would meet the love of my life through some melodramatic circumstance. Maybe I would even learn to smoke cigarettes! (Hey, I was twelve!) That wholesome welcome home note would surely bring me back to reality, no matter how jaded I had become.

Second, Mother insisted on a thorough housecleaning before we left. Daddy sympathized with us kids. Why clean house when we're leaving? But we certainly appreciated the order when we came home. Third, we made dozens of cookies to take along, just in case we couldn't afford any other food, I guess. Al Bell's favorite? Peanut butter with real peanuts in them. By the second week in New York, my brother Doug and I were feeding the stale things to the multitudes of pigeons that embellished the city like snowfall.

As usual, we drove long days, eating and sleeping in the car en route. Doug was almost eight, and we fought constantly. I couldn't stand his sticky touch on my sweaty body. I'd whine over the back seat, "Momma, Dougie's on my side again!"

Mother would reply rather absently, "Move over, Doug."

"Well, she's taking up more than her side, she's so fat!" (He knew I was overly sensitive about how I'd look in the movie and, of course, this gave me real confidence.)

"Take that back, you little brat! Momma, make him take it back!"

At this point, my dad would usually interject, "You kids BOTH sit by your windows or I'll stop the car!" Total silence from the back seat. We didn't get spanked often; we were very spoiled compared with our older brother and sister. As parents age, they become more lenient (read tired).

We arrived in New Jersey three days later. At dusk, Daddy pulled off the packed turnpike onto a peaceful, dead end road, so we could watch the sun set. "Mother, make us some sandwiches." Daddy had made an executive decision: we would "camp" one last night before hitting the city. I'm sure that decision had something to do with saving money, but it was so serene and pastoral, overlooking a grassy cow-dotted pasture, that we all agreed this was a good idea…until the sun went down. The humming began gradually, but within minutes the car was buzzing with vicious New Jersey mosquitoes. We swatted like crazy, rolled the windows up, and sweated out the night. I slept across the front seat, as usual, and banged my head (as usual) on the steering wheel every time I sat up to change positions. At the first hint of dawn, we gladly roared off to rejoin the busy procession into the great city.

Nothing in my young life so far had thrilled me as much as my first sight of the New York skyline. Photographs and imagination couldn't begin to prepare me for the overwhelming presence of those towering monoliths against the brilliant blue sky. The air had a slight fishy smell, mixed with a heavy industrial odor. Entering the long, dark, winding Holland Tunnel, our eyes gradually adjusted to the dim light of wall sconces, and many minutes later, the car emerged into the blinding daylight of our urban home for the next few weeks.

Mother had arranged for us to stay at the old Martinique Hotel on 34th and Broadway. Doug and I had never stayed at a hotel, period, so we were in for a treat. (Later visits revealed the Martinique to be rapidly deteriorating into a seedy, disintegrating establishment for questionable types, but in 1959, the hotel still exuded the posh glamour of its heyday.) Aging bellboys, uniformed in red jackets and caps, reminded us of the "Call for Philip Morris" boy from TV commercials. A grand red-carpeted staircase curved up from the lobby, and Mother prompted us to look up at the exquisite chandeliers. I labeled the hotel in my head as "fancy-schmancy," and stood a little taller.

Doug became enthralled with the elevator, the first self-operated elevator we farm kids had ever seen! (The rows of elevators at Younkers Department store in Des Moines were operated by stoic, uniformed, black ladies.) Doug watched Daddy push the appropriate buttons to open and close the door, and that elevator became his *raison d'etre* for the duration of our stay. Eventually, the manager asked Daddy to keep a closer eye on Doug. Any time we were in the hotel, Doug disappeared to "escort" guests up and down to their floors. He spent quite a bit of time alone in the elevator as well, which may have prompted more than one startled, overprotective woman to ask, "Where is your mother, little boy?"

"I don't know. What floor do ya want, lady?"

Our twelfth story room was actually rather depressing, but as our thrifty dad reminded us, "How much time are we going to spend in here?" It was small and dark with no view. One tiny window looked out on other hotel windows. For once, I had my own cot, so I didn't have to sleep with my hyper little brother. The hotel high point for me was the hallway window right outside our room. If I stood on my tiptoes, and leaned w-a-a-a-y out, I could see the Empire State Building in all its majestic glory! Of course, Doug had to see, too, so I would hold him up. The thought of us kids, precariously hanging out that window still gives me the willies.

The day we filmed from high atop the Empire State Building, I discovered that I have vertigo. Despite the high wire that kept me from being blown into the streets below, I still felt that plummeting feeling whenever I looked down at the "ants" below. How Greta was ever supposed to spot her grandpa from this elevation, only gullible grade-schoolers would know; indeed, she had to look down and be filmed doing it. It was terribly windy on the observation deck. The gusts almost blew my little brother over!

For the concluding scene there, Daddy directed me to look down to the streets below, turn back toward the camera, appear to be woozy from the height, and then collapse, as if I had fainted. We rehearsed it a couple times as tourists began to gather. I felt terribly self-conscious "acting" in front of those gaping strangers, but most of my paranoia was caused by that terrific wind blowing my skirt up and over my head! To Al Bell, time was money, of course, and he was getting this scene no matter what. The scene in "It's a Wonderful Life" when Jimmy Stewart's character finally breaks, and his daughter, the pianist, cries, "Oh, Daddy!" always reminds me of my struggle atop the highest building in the world. I was embarrassed to fall to the floor in front of all those strangers. Daddy coached, patiently, "Remember you're an actress. Ignore these folks, and let's try it again!" Al Bell rarely took three takes, but finally, exasperated, he growled, "This is your LAST chance, Becky! You better do it right!" However, on that final take, I didn't hold my prone position long enough. Feeling like a big, fat fool with my skirt blowing wildly around my shoulders, I broke character before Daddy yelled, "Cut!". Unfortunately, the camera, still running, filmed my eyes opening, my getting up, and then looking straight into the camera! I groaned every time I saw that scene in the finished movie. (I've always wondered if he left it in just to torture me for not "holding the moment.")

Now, I'm the sort of person who gets seasick in a rocking chair. So, although my stomach had been left behind when the express elevators tore upwards to leave us on top, it was nothing compared to leaving my innards on the observation deck as we plunged back to earth. Daddy's heart condition left him no choice but to feel sick. As he and I exchanged sickly, sympathetic looks, my mother and Doug, who both love roller coasters, just beamed at each other.

My sensitive equilibrium and stomach have had to endure slow ferries, too, on Al Bell trips. The Staten Island Ferry out to the Statue of Liberty didn't take nearly as long as the ferry rides on later trips, but Daddy and I still spent the entire trip at the bow, deeply inhaling the ocean air. I focused, not on my father's face, bobbing up and down beside me, but rather on the unmoving, gigantic woman with the torch, looming ahead. In those days, you could climb all the way up into her crown, which, of course, for an Al Bell movie, we had to do. Daddy was compelled to stop and rest frequently; the major hole in his heart had not yet been operated on. The stairs were narrow, dark and winding, but once we emerged at the top, the view between the vertical structures that made up the crown was breathtaking. I could see not only the sprawling metropolis that was New York City, but the island upon which it sprawled. The expanse of ocean was exhilarating.

Although we frequently ate homemade lunches in the hotel, our favorite eatery was the Automat. Automats may not be spectacular nowadays, but to us kids, they were as futuristic as Disney's Tomorrowland. The cold metallic décor and lack of interaction with humans (except for the cashier) seemed ultra modern. I ordered the same thing every day: an egg sandwich with tomato slices. Placing a quarter and dime into the coin slot, I watched in amazement as that clear, hinged window opened and "handed" me my sandwich. Ever the thriftiest of Scotsmen, Al Bell appreciated my cheap tastes. Mother and I were shocked, however, when he didn't refuse Doug's request for a luxury item – chocolate milk. Maybe it was Doug's impish grin when he piped up, "It's only a nickel, Daddy!" that made Al Bell give in.

Our budget did not allow for many "nice" restaurants. I remember two: a little Italian café where Doug and I were too cowardly to try anything but spaghetti, and a delightful, romantic Greek hideaway. The place was fairly empty, so the owner sat with us and told funny stories. The dark, handsome waiter kept winking at me, the music was strange and exotic, and Daddy and Mother laughed a lot. I have no idea what we ate, but that night, food took second place to ambience. Of course, my parents fulfilled their dream, experiencing Greece in person several years later.

Rockefeller Center took a whole day to film. After capturing the impressive art deco exterior, we took the NBC guided tour which included audience participation. We were shown how live sound effects were created, and we all got to clang bells and horse "clop" coconuts. A popular show at the time was a Bert Parks quiz show, "County Fair." I could almost tell what he looked like from the nosebleed section to which we were assigned. (I was impressed, nonetheless.) Since Daddy was carrying his film camera and tripod, the tour guide sternly warned him specifically not to film the TV show being taped live. "NO FILMING ALLOWED" never bothered Al Bell. If he wanted movies of something, he got movies. Daddy wasn't very sneaky, but he waited until the tour guide moved away, and from his lap, he aimed at the stage and shot a few frames of Bert Parks (later, the annual emcee of the Miss America pageant). The Queen Mother and Princess Paranoia were hissing, "Daddy!! She said", but Al Bell just kept shooting. Numerous times I pictured all of us behind bars, but Daddy was lucky with forbidden footage most of the time.

My mother, Chief of Trip Agenda, had found out about a Lions Parade, scheduled on Fifth Avenue, and since Miss America would be riding by, Daddy decided to film part of the parade. It was a balmy morning, and as usual, we took the bus up from our hotel. (Our car was never taken out of long term parking for this film.) We stood on the Central Park side of the street along with throngs of other pedestrians, and when Mary Ann Mobley (formerly Miss Mississippi) floated by, she beamed radiantly in our direction. She looked absolutely perfect, and once again, I was haunted by my sister's painful, but loving remark, "You could be Miss America, too, Susie, if you lost some weight." I realized on some level that my sister was probably biased, but whenever she called me , "Susie" (my character's name from the Okefenokee film), I vowed to stay out of the stale cookies.

Al Bell always needed something threatening or dangerous in his films, so he made contact with a policeman from Brooklyn whose beat was Harlem. The very nice policeman with the nasal, obnoxious accent invited us to his home where I met his daughter, a very nice girl about my age who also had a nasal, obnoxious accent. Of course, she said that I had the accent, but I'd heard that before, down south in Georgia!

I was surprised to find that the major difference between her home and most houses in the Midwest was that hers was extremely narrow with an extremely narrow yard. The two story house was actually quite large. I'll never forget sitting in the bathroom, peeking out between the window blinds, and realizing that there, just six feet away, was the neighbor's bathroom window! I considered not flushing the toilet, as even the neighbors would know what I was doing. While the very nice policeman took Daddy on a tour of tough Harlem neighborhoods and the precinct where he worked, the rest of us stayed with his family in Brooklyn. Daddy filmed an actual robbery in progress, and at the station, he was given permission to film confiscated weapons, like switchblades and sawed-off shotguns. With a few statistics on big city crime thrown into the later voiceover, Al Bell's "dangerous" day had been successful.

We used a couple other alternative modes of travel. A few streetcars were still running, and the electric poles and wires fascinated me. How did they do that? And the subway! We'd taken a subway to Brooklyn of course, and the speed and intermittent darkness were hypnotic. The fumes, we could do without. I recall taking a taxi only once. We needed to shoot the opening scene of Greta arriving on the ocean liner, and we had been given special permission to board and film the impressive "Independence." While we waited for Daddy to set up shots, Mother reminisced about their previous sailing trips until, despite my tendency to have motion sickness, I yearned to sail, too. The customs officials were likewise cooperative (thanks to Mother's early planning), and Daddy filmed Greta going through the long customs lines, so my immigrant status looked authentic.

A special highlight for me on this trip was our night on Times Square. We arrived around dusk, and the humidity was high. While we waited for the sun to go down, so Daddy could film the spectacular light show, we commented on the numerous novelty shops in the area. Being a curious group, we entered one nearby. This, surely, was the city at its seamiest. My wide eyes took in every risqué gift and gadget on the shelves: topless hula girls who shimmied on their little pedestals, sets of drinking glasses with obscene themes, and items featuring four letter words I'd never heard popped out at me from every direction. My very proper mother was horribly uncomfortable, but daddy ignored her protestations. His attention was directed to any potential gag gift he could take home to show Iowa. That limited the selection so severely that the shop owner himself was called upon to demonstrate his finest merchandise. He and Daddy laughed over hand buzzers and dribble glasses, but when the owner realized that Daddy wasn't going to invest more than a dollar or two, he made an abrupt exit. As I recall, the only purchase he made was a silly looking duck, which, when put near a glass of water, bobbed his long beak in and out of the water. Daddy loved it. Doug and I loved it. It was wholesome enough for Iowa.

Emerging from the last novelty shop, exactly at twilight, we were met by the most dazzling and colorful neon light display we could ever imagine. Gigantic signs advertising Coca-Cola and Marlboro cigarettes seemed to float and shimmer in the black nighttime sky. One brilliant marquee, in particular, held us in its spell for five minutes at a time, because it told a complete adventure story selling "Life" magazine. Daddy's camera recorded it for posterity, but the film didn't quite do Times Square justice. Had I been the theatre buff at the time that I was just six years later, I would have taken in the Broadway theatre marquees as well, but I do remember our parents steering us away from the "Girlie" burlesque shows and accompanying clientele.

A high point for Daddy on this trip was the Russian Exhibit. We were at the height of the Cold War, so this peek at real communists and their display of progress was indeed, educational.

It should be noted that, for all their bickering about what should be cut and what left in from the raw footage that was shot, my parents made quite a healthy balance when it came to the editing. Daddy lobbied for the scenes that were entertaining. After all, until he started the business of giving school assemblies, he had been an entertainer. "Happy Al Bell" was known and loved all over Iowa as a radio personality on WHO Radio, Des Moines, and from his barn dances and talent shows. As a former school teacher, my mother stood emphatically on the side of scenes that were educational.

"How can you teach them anything if they're bored with the movie?" Daddy would protest.

"I don't want to have to answer to superintendents who complain about the lack of teaching in the film!" Mother would counter.

So both my parents were thrilled to be filming all things Russian this day. Poor Doug was horribly bored and I was, too, at times, but I hated to admit it. I remember hearing Russian representatives speaking to other Russians in front of their respective displays, and fantasizing that I was in Russia. Such a difficult language it seemed, and so emotional! We gawked at their agricultural machinery – gargantuan combines, for example, that stood fifteen to twenty feet high. Daddy's John Deere paled in comparison. Mother and I were not so impressed by their fashions – drab uniform suits and dark, "plain Jane" dresses, bereft of any decoration. Doug and I walked and walked and stood and stood all day long and decided this was rather like the Iowa State Fair, except boring. Mother was in her dress and heels, of course, while Daddy carried all his equipment, so we were all exhausted by the time we got back to the hotel. But my parents were exuberant; they had filmed hours of pure education!

On several rainy days, Mother and Daddy stayed in the hotel, planning "What next?" while Doug and I repeated an adventure we had stumbled upon early in the trip. Thanks to the Christmas movie "Miracle on 34th Street", even folks outside of New York were familiar with Macy's and Gimbel's department stores. Our own Younkers in Des Moines seemed like Disneyland (Remember the Mezzanine? "Ladies Lingerie!"), but these were surely the Original Department Stores! Gimbel's was right across the street from the hotel, so it was permissible for us to be gone for an hour or two, as long as Mother knew generally where we were. (Different times, indeed…) The basic allure for us kids was not the merchandise or even the welcome air conditioning, but the escalators! Six floors were connected with escalators, and we traversed those moving stairs up and down, up and down, over and over. I must admit that Doug, with his elevator obsession, was a bit more smitten than I with escalators, but I did enjoy this mode of travel enough to hang with him for an hour or so. We'd ride in opposite directions, and "hail" each other when we passed:

"Hey, Becky! See ya on three!"

"Dougiee! See ya on four!"

Coming into view on the fourth floor, Doug would holler at me, "Becky Bell! What are YOU doing in New York City?"

"Hey! Aren't you Doug Bell? Al Bell's son?"

Eventually, I'd tire of the game and start window shopping, but I'd know exactly where to find my brother when it was time to go back to the hotel.

In later years, Daddy became more and more conscious of other people and their opinions, but especially when making movies, nothing was too outrageous. One afternoon, as we stood on a busy street corner waiting for the light to change, he got an idea. "Everybody look up!" he commanded us. Looking up, we saw nothing unusual, so we looked back at him questioningly. "Look up, and keep looking up, and see what happens..." Well, Daddy was the Boss, so naturally, we all looked up. Within seconds, people began to gather around us, all of them looking up. When a sizable crowd had formed, Daddy nudged Mother, then Doug and me. Daddy winked mischievously, and motioned for us to sneak out of the assembled throng. Crossing the street, we looked back, and there stood the "sheep" craning their necks upward in search of something that was not there. (They must have been tourists. New Yorkers would have known better.)

I vaguely remember our trip to Wall Street. Ominous brick buildings loomed over what seemed to be a particularly narrow street. The tour of the New York Stock Exchange culminated in a view through a floor to ceiling glass window, revealing the hubbub below. I couldn't imagine how anyone could possibly be heard in that tumultuous din! In fact, I'm still mystified.

We had all eagerly anticipated our day at the United Nations. After all, foreigners, with their exotic dress and strange languages, were our bread and butter. The open two-storied lobby featured the first of many colorful wall murals we would see. The theme seemed to depict some stage in the evolution of man's history, and I was mesmerized. Although there were no sessions scheduled that day, our guide took us inside and showed us the huge meeting rooms with dozens of labeled seats, representing more countries than I'd heard of in seventh-grade geography. As we observed the hundreds of dangling headphones, our young female guide, who was also a translator, explained how the translations were handled. She was quite firm in her instructions as to what Daddy was and was not allowed to film but as you can guess, Al Bell didn't take her seriously and took any footage that appealed to him. "This is for the kids in Iowa," he would always rationalize. "They deserve to see this." Because of Daddy's practiced poker face, Mother and I didn't even realize he'd been filming until we heard that unmistakable clicking of the camera in operation. We turned toward him, shocked and horrified that he'd so blatantly disobeyed the rules, but he was innocently smiling at our guide, nodding agreement with whatever she was saying while the camera pointed elsewhere.

As is typical of most guided tours, our last stop proved to be the gift shop; however, this was the gift shop of all gift shops! On crowded shelves, hand-painted tchochkes from all over the world demanded our attention. We all bought something, but my favorite item was forbidden to me, as Daddy had bought it for the program. The plump, colorful, wooden Russian peasant doll in her black shawl and red babushka, pulled apart to reveal another doll inside who had another smaller doll inside, who had another doll inside. Seven dolls in one deceiving package! I've seen these frequently since, but they were certainly novel back then.

After a month of purposeful sightseeing in this magical city, we were ready to shoot the reunion scene between Greta and her grandpa. Daddy had spotted a large settlement of brownstone buildings while filming in Brooklyn, and decided that this would be the ideal neighborhood for Greta's grandfather. Perhaps, he'd gotten the idea from the movie "A Tree Grows in Brooklyn." He was an avid fan of movies. He wanted all the front stoops to look identical. Panning down the street of seemingly cloned buildings, he shot a bewildered Greta, dazedly searching for her grandfather. Then, as happened frequently in scenes where Daddy became an actor, Mother took over the camera and followed Greta up to the only stoop where a white-haired old man with glasses sat dejectedly on the steps. "Gronpah?" she asked tentatively. Slowly, the old man looked up. "Greta?"

"OH, GRONPAH!!" I flew into my dad's outstretched arms. I felt very real emotion pass between us. Not because of any great acting on my part, but because of the poignant face and voice of Al Bell in character. I was sold, anyway, and I couldn't stop the little choke in my throat whenever that scene came up on the screen.

Daddy had such a flair for combining effective music with corresponding scenes. The last scene in the movie was shot in a park-like area across the street from the United Nations. A huge granite wall bore the inscription from the biblical passage, "We shall beat our swords into plowshares..." As the popular song by Irving Berlin with text by Emma Lazarus swelled in the background, we heard Greta call, "Hurry up, Gronpah!" Then I entered the picture, descending the steps in front of the inscription. Never one to miss an opportunity to pound out a message, my dad then zoomed in for a close-up of the words as I slowly walked out of the frame. It felt like a satisfying ending, and it was.

On our last New York morning, we redeemed our dusty car from hotel parking, and triumphantly drove out of the city. Looking back over my shoulder, I watched that famous skyline recede below the horizon, and I felt a huge lump rise up in my throat. "I don't want to leave!" I blurted out, and big tears splashed down my cheeks. Mother and Daddy assured me that someday I could come back on my own if I wanted, and I vowed then and there that I would.

Ten years later, I did, but that's another story.

**AL BELL**

*Proudly Presents*

**"Sons of New York City"**

WITH

Becky Bell as Greta  
Lions Int'l. Convention in N.Y.  
Russian Jet at Int'l. Airport

The Story of a Girl from Norway and her Search for her Grandfather in the Glamourous — Pathetic — Cynical — Exciting Surroundings of the Biggest City in the World.

See —
THE RUSSIAN EXHIBIT
NEW YORK STOCK EXCHANGE
CHINATOWN & HARLEM
THE UNITED NATIONS
BROADWAY AT NITE

& **LOTS MORE**

In New Eastman Ectachrome Color!

AL BELL PRODUCTIONS — STUART, IOWA

Becky Bell as Greta

## Chapter Seventeen

### "SONS OF ALASKA"

"We can't leave Itsy!" Doug wailed. Thus began the premise for yet another Al Bell movie. This would be our second trip to what was now our newest state. Al Bell was determined that the schoolchildren of Iowa should become more familiar with this faraway place of glaciers and Eskimos. I wrote myself my traditional welcome home letter and taped it to my bedroom door. "Dear Becky," it read. "I hope you had a good time and learned a lot about Alaska. Was it fun? Was it cold? Today is warm here, but not bad. I just got a permanent, so my hair will be easier to take care of on the trip. Gotta go, Becky."

"Itsy" was Doug's turtle. We never knew what sex it was, so Daddy and Doug christened it with a neutral name. With Doug's reminder of his hard-shelled pet, Daddy spontaneously began filming the beginning of our trip in the Bell driveway. Doug and I sat in lawn chairs, chatting artificially about our upcoming trip to Alaska. All I ever saw when that scene came up however, was my chopped off, frizzy hair – the last permanent of my lifetime! When Doug raised the issue of leaving Itsy, Daddy announced firmly from off camera, that the turtle was NOT going with us. Within four months, thousands of school children would see our red and white station wagon drive past the official "Welcome to Alaska" sign, as the camera panned to the highway below. Plodding laboriously behind the car, they would see a small turtle with "Itsy" painted in white on its shell.

We had thoroughly cleaned the house, moved all the plants to the basement, and packed the car, top to bottom with summer clothes, fall clothes, camera equipment and film, camping equipment, fishing equipment, medicine, games, and Chauncey. The aroma of Mother's wonderful chocolate chip and peanut butter cookies would waft through our air for days before she would allow us to have any. "They're going to have to last the whole trip, remember!" Doug and I, naturally, protested. "But they're the best now! They'll be stale by next week!" (In other words, hey, Mom, we've done this before, remember?)

Of course, we still camped in our (current) red and white stationwagon. As Doug and I had grown bigger and taller since the last trip though, Daddy came up with a double- decker bed plan. Doug and I slept (back to back) on the bunkbed mattresses on the folded-down seats, while our parents slept on their mattress, laid on a sheet of plywood, which was balanced on the rim of the windows about 15 inches above us. We rarely felt fresh air down there, but most nights were still cool. Now if you are trying to picture this, yes, in today's world, my parents would have put a curtain around the entire back of the station wagon. But there we were, sleeping four, sans curtains. It was crowded, but it worked.

It takes days to drive to Alaska from Iowa. Days and days and days. Our family always stops at historical markers, and, if a museum is affordable, we always go in. Our parents' philosophy was, "You'll only be here ONCE." Two summers before, on our way to Georgia, we had stopped at Rainbow Caverns, Tennessee – our first-ever cave tour. On our way through Montana, we stopped at the monument for "Custer's Last Stand" and we all sympathized with the Indians. Since we'd seen Lake Louise and Jasper/Banff Park on our way to Calgary for the 1955 film, "Sons of Chinook", we didn't stop, but did one of those whirlwind "There's a bear." "Where?" "It's gone now, you shoulda paid attention" drives through most of Alberta. The huge wheat fields around Calgary were quite a change of scenery for Doug and me, but after an afternoon of hot, dry riding, we became bored, and started bickering again. Occasionally, we lost Chauncey, but being a basset hound, our calls and his super sense of smell always led him back to the car. One entry from a notebook diary I kept for the first week and a half, tells of a typical car trip occurrence: "Chauncey spilled the turtle's sand on the blanket and sweatshirts." (The next sentence was about breakfast.)

At the Canadian border, we had to wait for the sun to shine so Al Bell could film Itsy, slowly crossing the official line. Though I haven't mentioned it much, the first priority when my dad was filming was Light. He always used a light meter. (What's a light meter? your

Al Bell as he looked for "Sons of Alaska"

children will ask.) We waited for hours sometimes on a cloudy day, just for enough of a sunbeam to light up the picture. In those days, campgrounds were a rarity, especially the further north we went. Daddy usually stopped for the night in abandoned schools or churchyards, but as the Yukon wilderness loomed ever nearer, he just pulled off the road wherever he could. From my diary: "Campgrounds stopped at the Alberta/British Columbia border, so we found a clearing in the forest. Played ball 'til eleven o'clock. It was so light!" On Friday, June 16th, I wrote, "Things getting real expensive! Sun goes down so late. It never really goes down – just gets kind of gray!"

Dawson Creek was officially Mile Zero of the Alcan Highway.

The impressive milepost monument in town gave distances to outlandish places like Peking, China and London, but the only distance we cared about was, "How many miles to Fairbanks?" The answer: 1, 486 miles! I couldn't believe it. We had already spent days that felt like weeks in our hot, packed car. Daddy filmed Doug, Chauncey and me. Mother had made a red terry cloth sweater for Chauncey that read, "Chauncey Bell". (It's interesting to note that in 1975, due to the metric changes going on in Canada, those historic mileposts were replaced, much to the disappointment of many American tourists.)

Traffic was spotty once we got on the Alcan (Alaska-Canadian) Highway. Sometimes we'd set up the tent (packed on top of the car with all our supplies), but too often we were too pooped, and crawled in with the mosquitoes. Daddy was the hero, of course, as he shut everyone else in, then came in last and sprayed vehemently while we hid our heads under the covers for a couple minutes. It's amazing my dad lived as long as he did, as he never mentioned his health in those days to get sympathy. I can't imagine how much pesticide residue we all have in our bodies from those reckless spray days. But the Northwest's mosquitoes are twice the size of Iowa's and twice as loud. Right before we all fell asleep, that familiar whine would start either upstairs or downstairs in our sleeping arrangement. You'd hear a slap, silence, whine, slap, silence, whine, until we'd either smashed the monsters or fallen into well deserved sleep.

Outside of Dawson Creek, we stopped for three days because our friends, the Danish Porsilds (who had put up the Bells in 1949) still ran a big, homey lodge. With the quiet forest rustlings, a nearby rushing river and big bridge, we totally relaxed and unwound. The lodge smelled of pine furnishings and fireplaces. The food was divine, covered with butter, sauces and gravies. "I really like Mr. Porsild's sister, "Toula" (from Greenland)." No wonder. She made us delectable Danish pastries every morning. The Porsilds were a very large, jovial bunch, and we all lingered at the long pine table, enjoying Daddy's stories and jokes. They asked about Rhea and Allen, who they remembered, of course, from the 1949 trip, but these kind folks couldn't get over how big I was. "You used to be so little and pretty!"

When they had last seen me, I was a blonde, curly haired, blue-eyed toddler, just "cute as a button." Now I was hazel-eyed, an ash blonde, and at that gangly stage, trying to rid myself of baby fat, by growing taller as fast as I could. It would have been tempting to have gorged on their huge, wonderful meals, but two teenage boys at the lodge had been eyeing me, so I suddenly had great will power. I hadn't had any boys interested in me yet, so this was rather titillating to my thirteen year-old hormones. The boys were with their families, of course, but for two nights straight, they walked me across the long bridge and back, while we chatted about everything and nothing. I hated leaving the next day, but bless their hearts, those two young men gave me my first self-confidence in regards to my looks.

Crossing the Canadian Rockies, we encountered hairpin turn after hairpin. There were a few guard rails, but not many. Daddy, always the daredevil, would wake us up once in a while by saying, "Look way down there, kids! You can see the river." And just as we leaned out our windows, Al Bell would swerve toward the edge, just a bit, to give us a better look. We were looking straight down a bottomless ravine, hundreds of feet below. Mother would scream, "Allen! Stop it!" He'd chuckle and drive more carefully for the next few miles. The roads were truly narrow on these switchbacks, and, on the rare occasions that we met a car going the other way, I held my breath. I knew my dad was an excellent driver, but it was a long, long ways down!

In Whitehorse, we saw three old steamboats, no longer in service, plus Sam McGee's cabin, made famous by Robert Service in the stark poem, "The Cremation of Sam McGee". Coming to Burwash Landing next, we saw an Indian cemetery. Whenever we reached a large town, we replenished our supplies of propane gas and groceries. If we had reason to go into a fairly civilized building, say a post office or gift shop, Doug and I would commiserate, "Don't you wish we could stay in here? Mom, Dad, we'll be here when you come back this way, OK?" We certainly revealed our spoiledness; we longed for the comforts of home already.

Shortly after we crossed the Alaska state line (photo op for Itsy), we stopped at the 40 Mile Roadhouse, where we saw Alaskan huskie pups, all blue-eyed. "We might get one," I wrote in my diary.

Daddy was an expert fisherman, especially fly fishing, so he caught a lot of tasty trout that Mother fried on our Colman gas stove, along with fried potatoes, of which Mother was a master. We had fried potatoes with scrambled eggs in the morning, and occasionally fried potatoes with hamburger when we finally found a grocery store. Mother also made chili and spaghetti with her second pan, an old pressure cooker. Otherwise, it was cold (sandwich) meat or peanut butter and jelly sandwiches in the car every day. Rarely did we eat in cafes, which were as rare as gold along the Alcan Highway back then.

We continued on to Fairbanks, an incredibly long stretch of nothing but pines, pines, pines. (My husband and I have chosen that type of topography today, having moved to Oregon, but thousands of trees, trees, trees were mighty tiresome back then.)

We met a young family, homesteaders, in a rare grocery store somewhere along the way, who were charmed by Daddy's manner, and they invited us to dinner. They lived way off the beaten path, but when we finally approached a big clearing, we knew we must be close. The husband got out of the car, then the wife with the baby and toddler, and gestured to us to move toward their car. "Where in the world is the house?" we were all wondering. He and his family walked to a slightly raised place on the ground, and he lifted up a sizable square board which became the entrance to their underground home! It was dark and damp and chilly, but once we'd been inside for awhile, I completely forgot we were underground. The wife thawed out some venison stew, heated it up, and served it with (stale) bread and butter, but it was very generous of them, nonetheless. Because of the perma-frost, their home had taken a couple of years to dig out, and they just weren't positive whether or not they'd build up above in the future. They liked the privacy, and more importantly, just in case there was a nuclear war (those were the scary years), they assumed they would be safe where they were. They had a radio, of course, which was on all the time.

Road construction was almost never ending. In fact there had been non-stop road construction ever since the Alcan highway was begun in 1942. It took until 1992 before the highway was finally finished, that is, paved. It took incredible patience for tourists to drive for hours at a maximum of forty miles an hour. If it had rained recently, and the road was a mire, a nearby truck would pull us through. Unfortunately, most of the time, we ate the dust of those trucks at ten to fifteen miles an hour. It took all day to get in a minimum of a couple hundred miles.

When we began to wonder where all the bears and moose were, Daddy would remind us, "With all this construction noise going on, why would they stand next to the road? They have thousands of miles to wander without even coming close to this highway." In the areas without construction, however, it became our responsibility to find wild animals. There was no reading, no laptops, no movies. Daddy had trained us well to spot deer and bears, of course, but we learned to look for moose in lowland swamps called muskeg. At the higher elevations, we stopped frequently, in case we could spot an occasional grizzly bear or big horn sheep. Al Bell's movies had to boast plenty of wildlife, so it became a competition. Daddy had the best eyes among us, but Doug and I were quite proud to have found good animal scenes that would be used in the movie. Mother surprised herself, by spotting the first grizzly bear.

A community of sorts emerged from those of us who were traversing Alaska. Case in point: a particular dark blue station wagon had passed us, and then let us pass them for a couple days in a row on the long road to Fairbanks. Steep, narrow switchbacks (or bobbypin curves, as I called them) set the scene for these passing maneuvers one day. About the third day that we passed our "friends," Doug leaned out the window, and yelled at them, "IT'S A GAME!" We all exploded in laughter as we left them behind again.

I'm sure there are Motel 6's and Denny's dotting the Alcan Highway now, but we didn't get to eat regularly at all on those interminably lonely roads. One day, we had arisen from our camp site, particularly hungry, and anxiously looked for the first restaurant or café we could find. About an hour later, we pulled into the parking lot of a very busy eating establishment with visions of pancakes and eggs dancing in our heads.

Doug and I hadn't unwedged ourselves yet from the bed below, when Daddy yelled out, "Kids! Stay in the car! We're going on right away!" Now what? Obviously, it had to be wild animals up ahead. Since we hadn't seen any bighorn sheep yet, Al Bell was not about to miss them now. Another couple hours up the road, we parked on the shoulder behind a long line of cars. We all scrambled up the side of a rocky mountain to the point where Daddy could use his zoom lens to capture a herd of Dalls, balancing on tiny precipices. Several other tourists, cameras in hand, perched on the side of that mountain, so we knew that no one else had spotted any Dalls up to that point, either.

The day continued, just as furiously as it had begun. "Grizzlies up ahead!" a photographer yelled at us. We had just stopped to relieve ourselves behind some big rocks, and now it was, "Mother, Becky!

Hurry up and get back to the car!" This was the kind of day that we liked, of course, because it went fast, but Doug and I were getting hungry. Onward we drove, catching great shots of a grizzly family down below the road on a ledge that overlooked a long valley. Thank goodness for the invention of the zoom lens. We could make them out with binoculars, but Daddy's zoom captured a huge, reddish mother and two roly-poly cubs romping around her for the movie.

Although I have fond memories of these trips and the experiences they provided, they were certainly not, nor were they meant to be, family vacations. Daddy's word was our command. If we had to go to the bathroom, but we spotted a moose first, guess which took priority? We Bell kids got used to it, but on this particular day, it was nine o'clock at night when we stumbled, hungry and weary, into a rough log cabin café just off the road across from scenic Dot Lake. A friendly, rather sassy older woman called out, "There ain't nothin' left but pie." All of us had been anticipating big, juicy hamburgers.

"Really? You don't have anything but pie?" my mother asked. Doug and I were famished, but we were almost more tired than anything else. When four pieces of cherry pie came to the table, we sat for a second and yawned, before reaching for our forks. My nine-year old brother stared at his pie for a moment longer, and said to me from out of the side of his mouth, "Some breakfast!"

Forest fires had decimated thousands and thousands of forested acres along several stretches of the Alcan Highway . The majority of these were caused naturally, but the highway signs of Smokey the Bear, wearing his ranger hat, numbered in the hundreds. The message was always the same, "ONLY YOU CAN PREVENT FOREST FIRES." One day, in particular, scenery consisted only of acres of blackened toothpicks as far as the eye could see. We felt really bad about it, at first, particularly because of all the forest creatures who had obviously not survived these fires, but by late afternoon, Doug and I were yearning for the green trees again. It was a mighty depressing sight. We even saw live embers still burning in one or two places. Obviously, no wild animals would emerge from this deadened terrain, and even Daddy became impatient to get to Fairbanks.

The outskirts of Fairbanks in 1960 looked like a pioneer town in a western movie – dark, wooden buildings, cabins, lots of saloons with swinging doors, and riders on horses. Daddy followed signs which got us to the S.A.C. base which was thrilling, but frightening.

With a Cold War going on, and Russia just across the Bering Strait, Al Bell felt that these were important scenes.

Daddy had planned to take a flight to Nome, Kotzebue, and ultimately, Point Barrow, the northernmost "city" (actually an incorporated settlement of mostly Eskimos) in North America, so he found us a place to spend the three days he would be gone. After driving around for awhile, he found what he was looking for. Just outside of town, he had decided a safe (and cheap) refuge would be a sewage plant set in a sort of park-like area…memories of Waycross, Georgia. We didn't know any better. Doug and I were kids raised on a farm who needed a pond and some space. Health issues aside, we blissfully floated in sewage water, as Mother called out every so often, "Watch out for rusty tin cans!" Obviously, when we found them, it was too late, but she doctored us with her trusty Merthiolate and Band-Aids. It was freeing, not adhering to any harried schedule – ala Al Bell. Mother kept us busy with sightseeing in Fairbanks, too.

We went to the University of Alaska museum next where we were greeted at the top by the giant of all bears, a ten-foot Kodiak bear on its hind legs. (Stuffed, of course.) Exhilarating feelings of fear mixed with awe rushed over me, and I wanted to stay and study him, but a group of tourists behind us compelled us to move on into the museum. In addition to many bears, including polar bears, the fairly primitive dioramas showed arctic foxes, wolves, otters, seals, walrus, elk, caribou, and moose with five foot wide racks of tree branch size antlers. Fortunately, I had matured enough to appreciate all the relics from gold discovery days and primitive Eskimo clothing and housing. The time passed quickly for me, but Doug was nine years old and very bored.

On our way to Fairbanks, we had been reading the billboards advertising "Jonas Brothers Museum of Taxidermy so many miles ahead" for hours, so that was our next stop. They had a huge, stuffed polar bear, and an Eskimo village diorama. Returning to the sidewalk below, I began to people watch. The taxi drivers, a pretty sleazy looking lot, whistled and made cat calls at me. Sure, I was repulsed by their looks – hairy, bearded, dirty jacketed – but this was all new and exciting to be noticed. When one guy on the street approached me from behind, close enough to whisper an obscene remark, I quickened my step, caught up with my family, and thanked God I was only thirteen. Too much information.

By the third day, we kids were ready to move on, and Mother

was lonesome for her husband. We had eaten and slept in the car, so the only break she got from us was our daily swims in the algae pool. And, it was chilly. We rarely shed our jackets or sweatshirts, as the temps ran sixty to maybe seventy degrees in the daytime, and forty to fifty at night.

Finally, the time came to retrieve Daddy from the Fairbanks airport. We jumped up and down around him, as Mother embraced him. At last! We could continue on with this challenging (read LONG) adventure. As we finished grocery shopping for the long journey ahead, Daddy filled us with news of his trip. For eight extra dollars, he got to fly over Big and Little Diodema, and took footage of Siberia in the distance. Point Barrow was mostly an Eskimo community with melting ice on two sides, and Daddy was grateful that he had splurged on a beautiful authentic Eskimo parka. "I would have frozen without it!" he admitted. He had shared many stories of the people he met, and the footage he had taken before he interjected, "Oh, yeah. I took this sled ride with Huskies pulling the sled, and I got the seat in front. Well, we were out somewhere, and the driver stopped, and this dog right in front of me turned around and bit me." Total silence while we absorbed this information. I had formed a furrow in my unwrinkled brow, when Mother interrupted.

"Al Bell! Say that again, the part about bitten by a sled dog."

"Oh, yeah. I don't know why, I didn't do anything to provoke him. You know me; I like dogs."

"What happened after he bit you?" Mother pressed. "Did you tell anybody? Did anybody do anything for you?"

"Oh, yeah", he answered casually. "The airlines said they'd replace my trousers, and said not to worry about rabies. Oh, and they wanted to know where to get a hold of us."

"Allen! Do you think the sled dog had rabies? Because we've got to see a doctor if – "

"I'm fine. Just fine." And he dismissed it as if it were yesterday's weather.

Movies of Mt. McKinley (now referred to as Denali) were an absolute must for the program, of course, since it is the highest mountain in the Western Hemisphere. Naturally, Daddy put snippets of "Itsy", plodding along the highway behind us. We proceeded south from Fairbanks to Denali National Park which began to climb steadily higher, until we saw more of a tundra landscape. Prairie dogs bounced in and out of a jillion holes, and a gray fox walked right down the road in front of the car. As we drove ever higher, snow drifts on either side of the road came into view. Doug and I couldn't believe our eyes: sizeable snowdrifts in June! Al Bell never missed an opportunity, so Doug and I were told to change into our shorts, stand in the snow barelegged, and throw snowballs at each other. It was plenty cold, but we were ordered not to look cold, of course. "Smile! Laugh!" ordered our director. It was so hard to remember Iowa's warm weather going on, just several thousand miles away. Mount McKinley wasn't evident until we were about fifty miles away, but coming over a hill, that giant mountain of ice and snow loomed on the horizon, shimmering, like a mirage.

That night, I wrote excitedly in my diary that we stayed in a "sprayed campground". The next morning we came to Sable Pass where we saw Dall sheep above us When we came down, we drove around the next corner where a sign was posted: "Do not get out of car or off road for next five miles because of grizzly bears." A couple miles up the road, we saw Dall sheep again on the sides of mountains. Suddenly, a tourist near us yelled something, and we saw, on the other side of the road, hundreds of caribou! We heard later that there were an estimated six hundred. Daddy had to wait quite awhile before he got a clear shot of Mt. McKinley, and five minutes later, clouds surrounded the peak again. From there we went to Wonder Lake and then the road to Denali Camp. Note: I tried to follow our trip on the maps of a 2008 Milepost magazine, but couldn't find some of these names. They are written in my diary, nonetheless.

We were now on our way to Skagway and Juneau with planned attractions on the way, so we tended to put any questions over Daddy's health out of our heads, temporarily. Mother, however, would bring up the problem at least once a day. "How do you feel, Allen?" And my smart-alec dad would foam at the mouth or act crazy for a minute, just to bug her.

We didn't stop as often southward, except for Bridal Veils Waterfall. Daddy had spotted it from quite a distance away; the falls shimmered in the afternoon sun. Al Bell waited for just the right angle to get the most impressive view of this long wedding veil of water, and as we stopped, we could hear the thundering roar from several miles away. Thank goodness, that meant everyone got a potty break, and though Mother and I hated squatting behind trees, rocks and in emergencies, an open car door, it was still better than the alternative.

Mother related her only naughty joke in those moments. In fact, she had recited it on special occasions since she was little (and barely understood the punch line):

A little boy and girl wander away from the family picnic to relieve themselves. She observes him from behind a tree, and calls out, "Gee, I wish I had a picnic gadget like that!" As I recall, my mother always blushed when she told it, but she repeated it regularly on trips, anyway. It was just too appropriate.

Haines was definitely windy and chilly, but we arrived in time to watch the intricate and colorfully costumed Chilkat Indian dancers performing for a local festival. Some of the men were barely clothed; I mention that only because it was cold. Haines was the first port we had visited, and my mother complained about the fishy smells. I could never make up my mind if I really loved ocean air, or if it was the pungent smell of fish. Having lived by the ocean, I now realize that the fishy aroma of bays and harbors come from the docks and the canneries, not from the ocean…duh. And I definitely prefer the ocean air! Somewhere in our journey (the answer is in the movie), Daddy was given permission to film at a big cannery. He began with the various stages of salmon fishing to the men tossing the fish onto conveyor belts, to the folks on the pier who prepared the fish for canning. We followed him around, and the odor was magnificent. As salmon is my favorite meal now, I'm sure I was smitten way back then.

In Skagway, Daddy took footage of Eskimos and totem poles, including an authentic Eskimo wedding ceremony in progress. The bride wore a plush, sable parka. I didn't notice the groom. Skagway sits on an inlet of the bay north of Juneau. From there, we took a ferry to Alaska's capital.

*Mal de mer*, or seasickness, is preventable nowadays. The ferry ride is perhaps one of the most beautiful in the world, but I didn't enjoy much of it. I wanted to die. After standing at the rail for hours, expecting to heave over the side at any time, Mother suggested she take me to the restroom, where I did throw up – in the toilet, in the sink, and on the floor – for the rest of the trip. Poor Mother kept cleaning up after me. Once in a while, she'd disappear to let Daddy know where we were; he and Doug were having a wonderful time on deck.

Through my recovering stupor, about all I remember of Juneau are totem poles. Millions of them. As the sun was setting, we approached the suburbs of Juneau. A rather primitive park full of totem poles invited us to explore, and the poles were fascinating. Some were the size of enormous trees (which they were) and close to fifteen to twenty feet high. Daddy listened patiently to my query regarding how they carved up "that high".

"They carve them on the ground."

"Oh!"

After having seen the impressive gold dome on top of the Iowa State Capital Building (our sixth grade class got to climb up inside the dome), the Alaska capitol building and city itself seemed primitive. Many residents lived in cabins, but a great deal of construction was going on.

I remember the isolated, history-laden town of Sitka. Sitka was capital of Russian Alaska until the year 1900, and, to my adolescent mind, it felt like Russia. The few citizens we saw were dressed in early twentieth-century clothing. Today, I would describe them as looking like extras from "Fiddler on the Roof." The only attraction that has stayed vividly in my mind is a Russian Orthodox Church built in the 1880s. It was still being used on a regular basis. And the door was open! We went in, and I gaped at all the icons and finery, and tried to understand that these folks worshipped the same God that we did back at St. John's Lutheran in Casey. The onion-shaped dome was new to my experience in 1960, but it has become one of my favorite architectural shapes.

Wild animals were harder to find now, but the scenery was absolutely awesome. Outside of Juneau, we followed signs to Mendenhall Glacier which was the closest we got to a real, mammoth, frozen snow drift. We stood directly across from it on the lake shore. It seemed that it was only yards away. Its radiance, which was almost hard to look at in the sun, reflected onto the clear, icy lake below. Chilly, yes, but Al Bell directed Doug and me to change into tee-shirts and shorts for yet another scene of us making and throwing snowballs at each other. Remember, you didn't say "No" to my father.

Perhaps I should clarify the biggest difference between our film trips and other trips. If we kids impaired the progress of the film in any way, we were directly affecting our ability to eat and wear clothes that fall and winter. Maybe more children should be involved in their parents' livelihoods. It certainly brings reality into focus. All of us kids were responsible for paying as much of our college tuitions as possible: my sister and I both worked several summers at Camp Okoboji when we were in high school, and then we worked switchboard in our respective dorms at college. My older brother Allen sold encyclopedias in Des Moines and worked on construction crews who were making Interstate 80 a reality. My brother Doug worked several jobs, including hauling garbage on the south side of Des Moines. We all de-tasseled corn and worked in bean fields, of course. Our parents made it obvious from the time we were young that there was no free ride. They both had worked to go to college, and so would we.

With so few real highways in Alaska at that time, we spent a lot of time back-tracking. Coming back from southeast Alaska, we saw few surprises until we headed south for Seward. Daddy kept telling us that we were very close to the ocean, but not until we reached the Kenai Peninsula did we smell and feel ocean air. The history of Seward began with Russian explorers, fishermen and trappers, but the city is best known now for the Iditarod Sled Dog Races.

Driving back north as we were leaving Seward, Daddy remarked that we better get gas again, so we stopped at a station and filled it up. Gas prices were unbelievable – over a dollar a gallon some places, while at home in Iowa, gas was only 25 cents per gallon. We all got out, stretched, and bought a soda pop while Daddy made friends with the owner/attendant. We were just pulling out of the station, when we heard the man holler, "STOP! STOP!" He was motioning for us to come back.

"Who? Us??" We couldn't understand what he was yelling, but he was visibly upset, so Daddy slowed down and turned around.

Then we could hear him, "YOU'RE THE MAN WHO HAS RABIES!!" Our mouths dropped open, as Daddy pulled back into the gas station. Mother was out like a flash.

"WHAT ARE YOU TALKING ABOUT?!"

"Calm down, Mother, let me talk to the man," Daddy said as he approached the man.

"It was just on the radio. They've been looking for a man who was bitten by a rabid sled dog in Point Barrow a few days ago. It's YOUR license plate number! You've got to drive to Anchorage immediately to get the shots!"

The station owner called the highway patrol to say that we were on our way, and they promised a police escort as soon as we reached

Anchorage. We had only hours left before Daddy would turn into a wild man, foaming at the mouth. Mother, Doug and I were petrified with fear, but Al Bell just laughed about it and made jokes. I realized later that this was his way of hiding his own fear, and quelling it in others. It's a smart survival technique that some folks pick up on, and others don't – like my poor mom, who understandably panicked to think we'd been casually driving around Alaska when there was a deadline on my dad's life.

Thus, a race against time began that didn't stop until we'd found the hospital in Anchorage. No sight seeing or stopping for this leg of the journey; we had a mission, and Daddy barely let us stop to go to the bathroom for the next few hours. The only fact that our folks were aware of, and dreading, was the agonizing procedure of getting the shots: Daddy would receive fourteen injections in his abdomen. Doug and I couldn't even imagine undergoing fourteen shots, let alone in our tender bellies. Mother got teary, but assured Al Bell that she would hold his hand for every one of them. And she had to. Doug and I were left in the outer lobby for what seemed like hours. When they finally returned, Daddy looked as weak as a wet kitten. Later, after we got back home, we were told that the radio bulletins about finding Daddy were sent all the way back through Canada to Iowa, and my brother Allen had heard the news before we did!

Fortunately, we had planned to go to Anchorage next, anyway. The next morning, Daddy was up to shooting scenery and downtown pictures. A few years back, in the mid-1980's, I met a nice young man at an acting workshop in Los Angeles who had grown up in Anchorage. John had vivid memories of the 1964 earthquake that was centered in his hometown. He told me that he had been playing in the back yard, when suddenly, the ground beneath his feet moved violently, and he was knocked several feet away, flat on his back. Being a Midwesterner, I found it difficult to even imagine an earthquake, and I thanked God that the scariest weather we faced was tornadoes back in Iowa.

We had to stay in Anchorage for a couple days just to make sure that Daddy's recovery was complete. His stomach was swollen and terribly sore, and as a result, we didn't hang out any longer in the city than we had to. But it was so nice to be in a city again! I had no illusions of coming back to play pioneer here, but I have wanted to return as a tourist someday. On Al Bell trips, we filmed scenes only where Daddy thought his school kids would be interested. I've been asked many times if I saw such and such a place, and when I admitted I had not, the questioner asked the inevitable, "You haven't? You can't be serious! EVERYBODY goes to " Not with Al Bell, you didn't.

Daddy had plenty of footage by this time; it was a standing rule. When he ran out of film, it was time to go home. Rarely, did he call home for additional film to be sent to his location. Besides, Daddy was anxious to stop spending money and get home to catch up on his farm responsibilities.

We really put in long days now. At least 500 miles per day were required by the Boss, who never let Mother drive back then. The homemade cookies were too stale for any of us but Mother, who always sacrificed, so as not to waste anything ! "Now, these are just fine," she'd say as her teeth worked to bite off a stale piece. Eventually, Daddy would down a few of his peanut butter cookies, but Doug and I just broke the chocolate chip cookies apart, and ate the chocolate. Of course, we had already seen all this scenery, so we napped a lot in the back while our parents talked quietly in front.

Daddy had just enough film to shoot a couple more clips of the film's star, Itsy, plodding slowly across the Canadian border, and eventually, the Iowa state line. Four weeks after we had left Menlo, we walked back into our hot, stuffy, dark house. I read that naïve note, taped to my bedroom door. "Yes, it was cold at times, especially compared to here," I thought to myself. "Was it fun? Well, once in awhile." But I had to admit, Alaska was very impressive. And it felt very far away now. I touched my grown out frizzy hair, and ran back to the kitchen where Mother was unloading food. "Please, please, please, can I get my hair cut REAL short tomorrow?"

Oh, yes! The folks in Point Barrow dutifully shot the dog that they thought had bitten Daddy and sent its head to Fairbanks for analysis. However, there had been a mix-up between two separate sled dogs. A second dog had developed rabies after Daddy left Point Barrow. The medical results awaited us at home. The report verified that the dog who had actually taken a fair chunk of my Dad's leg did NOT have rabies after all.

## Chapter Eighteen

Our high school years rushed by, packed with sports, plays, speech contests, and recitals, and our devoted mother was always in attendance. Daddy came as often as he could, considering his busy schedule. As much as Mother objected to the limited education a small school could offer, she finally decided to do something about it – she ran for the school board. In time, Rhea Bell became the first woman president of the Menlo school board. Several strong women in the community supported her: Virginia Van Duzer, the best teacher Menlo ever had; Alice Groomes, who through Mother's efforts, taught French, the first foreign language ever offered at MHS, and dear Mary Cashman, whose friendship kept Mother going through frustrating times. For an appropriate social outlet, a bridge club was formed, made up of teachers and other friends in the community. On those nights, Doug and I stayed in our rooms without complaint.

After her last child enrolled in college, Mother made Daddy keep his promise; he sold the farm so Mother could return to a city life. Al Bell's health had been compromised anyway, by trying to balance the responsibilities of keeping a farm afloat and keeping up with his full school schedule. He gave in to the move without much of a fight. I, on the other hand, was terribly disappointed. So was Doug. Our reasons were purely selfish, of course, because we were too blind to see how much Mother had sacrificed to give us our idyllic life on the farm. I was upset, however, when my mother wrote me that she and Daddy had held an auction – past tense – of almost everything, our personal things included. My first teaching job kept me in Lewiston, Minnesota, that year, but if I had known about the auction beforehand, I would have driven nonstop to rescue my childhood from my bedroom closet.

Nonetheless, we kids visited our parents in Ankeny, then to Breezy Heights on Lake Okoboji, and lastly, Arizona, where they retired.

The Al Bells couldn't stop giving programs cold turkey, however. Daddy and Mother scheduled a few programs in Arizona elementary and middle schools the first few years that they were "snowbirds" (part time Arizona residents). After they moved to Green Valley, a growing retirement community south of Tucson, my parents still gave a few programs at their church. Did you know that of all the retirees who move to Arizona, Iowans are the most represented state? As a result, Al Bell was frequently recognized by fellow Iowans not only at church, but at Walgreens!

My parents created a legacy, I am proud to say, that valued Travel as a valid course of study for life. Thousands of Iowa school children who experienced Al Bell programs learned geography, cultures and customs, foreign dress and thought, history, and more. And that education came to them in the most palatable method: entertainment. Daddy received several awards over the years, from the Iowa State Education Association to the Kiwanis. Because the awards were given to Al Bell the Educator, my parents treasured them more than anything they had collected from sixty-five countries visited over a span of thirty years.

One of the many, many postcards Mother sent to me over the years.

Becky Bell-Greenstreet | 137

*Al Bell*
- presents -

"SONS of HOLLAND"

KENYA

The Al Bells

The Al Bells send Christmas Greetings from The Holy Lands

School 'reminder' cards and Christmas cards from 'The Al Bells' around the world.

AL BELL PROUDLY PRESENTS!
"SONS OF MOROCCO"
SADDLEMAKER
POTTER
AL IN ACTION
CAMELS
STORKS
DONKEYS
WATER WHEELS
VEILED WOMEN
HOODED ARABS
WALLED CITIES
ROMAN RUINS
ALONG THE ROAD
AL BELL PRO
"Let's Go Dutch"
AL BELL'S WORLD
On a Happy Holiday to
With the Al Bel
SONS OF HOLLAN
Vollendam
THE AL BELLS
A Canal Trip
"Madurodam" Little Peoples World
ZY HEIGHTS, MILFORD, IOWA
AL BELL'S WORLD
See the Islands on the Equator where
Darwin's Theory started!
Galapagos Tortoise
Land Iguana
Al Bell
Colorado Indian
Blue Footed Boobies
Seals
TOWER
JAMES
SANTA CRUZ
ISABELA
SAN CRISTOBAL
FLOREANA
HOOD
EXPLORE
with Al Bell
THE STRANGE AND WEIRD
WORLD ON THE EQUATOR
SONS of GALAPAGOS
AL BELL PRODUCTIONS - BREEZY HEIGHTS, MILFORD, IOWA
Spend a Se
AL BELL'S WORLD
In Sunny
"SONS OF SPAIN'
The Al Bells
Don Quixote's Windmill
BULLFIGHTING SPAIN'S NATIONAL SPORT
Flamenco Dancers
Corpus Christi Parade
Columbus' Tomb
28th Year
AL BELL PRODUCTIONS - MILFORD, IOWA
AL BELL says
Definitely My Most Thrilling Trip
"SONS OF PERU"
SIX TIMES ACROSS THE ANDES!
FARMING AT 15,000 FT.!
IN THE JUNGLE ALONG THE AMAZON!
LLAMAS ON THE HIGH PAMPAS.
WORLD'S MOST PRIMITIVE PEOPLE.
THE CROWNING OF THE INCA
(ALL IN BEAUTIFUL COLOR AND SOUND)
AL BELL PRODUCTIONS — STUART, IOWA

# Film List

## AL BELL'S TRAVELS

1949 "Along the Alcan Highway" (Alaska)  The Bell family, scenery/animals
1950 "Sons of Scandinavia" (Sweden, Norway, Denmark) Daddy and Mother
1951 "Sons of the Tropics" (Central America: Guatemala, Nicaragua, Honduras)
Allen stars; Daddy is the mysterious stranger.
1952 "Sons of Gaspe" (Nova Scotia & Quebec, Canada) The family is featured in this creative, artsy film.
1953 "Sons of the West Indies" (Haiti, Cuba, Jamaica) Mother and Daddy are followed.  Voo-doo intrigue.
1954 "Sons of Ireland"  Daddy follows a treasure map left by his Irish ancestor
1955 "Sons of Chinook" (Alberta, Canada, Banff Jasper Nat'l Park, Calgary Stampede)  Allen starred with Maggie, our basset hound, and Daddy was the villain.  Allen uses a Geiger counter to find uranium.  Cowboys & Indians.
1956 "Sons of Austria"  Daddy plays the absent-minded professor in search of musical inspiration.  Mother played the coquettish Austrian girl at the end.
1957 "Sons of Okefenokee" (Waycross, Georgia)  Becky stars as a spoiled, little rich girl who dumps the tour guide (Daddy) and gets lost in the swamp.  Mother played her snooty mother.  Doug has a cameo.
1958 "Sons of Hawaii" Mother starred as a teacher on vacation.  Daddy played the mysterious stranger.
1959 "Sons of New York City" Becky starred as a Norwegian immigrant, searching for her grandfather in the Big Apple.  Daddy played "Grandpa".
1960 "Sons of Alaska"  Doug and Becky are featured, as well as Doug's turtle, Itsy and our family dog, Chauncy.

1961 "Sons of Morocco" Mother and Daddy and Mohammed Busseta, guide
1962 "Sons of Newfoundland" Doug and Becky look for their grandfather in Newfoundland.
1963 "Sons of Peru" Highlight: Rhea and Al lived with the primitive Shipibo Indians deep in the Amazon jungles. Their hosts: Louise and John MacGregor, missionaries.
1964 "Sons of Florida" Daddy and Doug star in this search for the Fountain of Youth.
1965 "Sons of the Holy Land" Daddy plays the mysterious "Sheik". Emphasis on Biblical places and religious history.
1966 "Sons of Scotland" Emphasis on our Bell ancestry
1967 "Sons of Portugal"
1968 "Sons of Africa" (Kenya) *Mother joins lecture, due to Daddy's health
1969 "Sons of Greece"
1970 "Sons of Hong Kong"
1971 "Sons of Galapagos" (Ecuador and the Galapagos Islands)
1972 "Sons of Romania" Daddy starred as "Count Dracula" of Transylvania
1973 "Sons of the Navajo" (Navajo Tribe and Chief Peter MacDonald in Northern Arizona)
1974 "Sons of Holland"
1975 "Sons of Spain"
1976 "Sons of Egypt"
1977 "Sons of Shipibo" (Daddy and Mother remade the Peru film — Daddy's health)
1978 Transfer to Warren Grant; Daddy and Warren did that year together